Grace, Love and Holy Spirit

A Growing in the Word Series

by the elevateHim Team

Distributed by elevateHim Ministries
P.O. Box 2554
Fort Worth, TX 76244
817-431-3336
www.elevatehim.com

ISBN: 978-1-7327791-0-5

All rights reserved. Published in the United States of America
Publication graphics, layout and cover designs by elevateHim Team.

Contents

Week 1 - The Trinity   1
Day 1 - God the Father   3
Day 2 - The Sin that Separates   6
Day 3 - Jesus the Son   10
Day 4 - Holy Spirit is the Ultimate Gift-Giver   13
Day 5 - Open the Gift   16
Day 6 - The Purpose of Rest   19

Week 2 - Faith by Grace   21
Day 1 - Grace is the Lens of Love   23
Day 2 - Grace and Faith Work   26
Day 3 - Grace Not by Works   29
Day 4 - Grace Over Judgment   32
Day 5 - Grace Gives Identity   36
Day 6 - Resting in Grace   39

Week 3 - Word of God Speak   43
Day 1 - The Word in the Beginning   45
Day 2 - The Word Is Alive and Active   48
Day 3 - Hide God's Word in our Hearts   51
Day 4 - The Old and New Testament   54
Day 5 - How to Study the Word   57
Day 6 - Resting My Mind   60

Week 4 - Hearing God   63
Day 1 - Hearing God through Prayer   65
Day 2 - God Speaks, We Listen   69
Day 3 - Hearing God Through His Word   73
Day 4 - Hearing God Through His Spirit   78
Day 5 - Hearing God Through His People   82
Day 6 - Resting in His Creation   87

Week 5 - The Cross

Day 1 - The Story of the Cross ... 93
Day 2 - Salvation Through the Cross ... 95
Day 3 - Grace and the Cross ... 99
Day 4 - The Finished Work of the Cross ... 103
Day 5 - The Resurrection Power ... 107
Day 6 - Resting in the Cross ... 111

Week 6 - Sin and the Real Enemy

Day 1 - Sin is Missing the Mark ... 115
Day 2 - Sin isn't the Focus ... 117
Day 3 - We are Already Forgiven ... 120
Day 4 - Exchanging Lies for Truth ... 122
Day 5 - Exchanging Our Wrong Believing for Grace ... 127
Day 6 - Resting Our Physical Bodies ... 130

Week 7 - Our Identity

Day 1 - We are Sons and Daughters of God ... 135
Day 2 - We are a New Creation ... 137
Day 3 - We are His ... 139
Day 4 - We Have a Purpose ... 142
Day 5 - We Live by Faith ... 146
Day 6 - Resting in Joy ... 149

Week 8 - Living in Relationships

Day 1 - My Relationship with God ... 155
Day 2 - My Relationship with Myself ... 159
Day 3 - My Relationship with Others ... 162
Day 4 - Healing Broken Relationships ... 166
Day 5 - Living Like Relationships Matter ... 171
Day 6 - Resting in Peace ... 174

Appendix

(1) Salvation Letter ... 177
(2) Baptism ... 178
(3) Your Guide to Communion ... 178

About Fully Alive

... 181

Dear Friends,

We are honored you chose to embark on this journey with us. Wherever you are, right now, is a great place to be and we can't wait to walk arm-in-arm with you as you grow in your love for the Father, embracing and understanding His love, nature and character.

One thing that we've discovered, is everyone on the face of this planet needs encouragement. We have been personally encouraged while developing this book and our prayer is that each of you would be encouraged as well. Our hope is that as you go through the pages in this book you encounter, experience and have a full-on relationship with God the Father, The Son and The Holy Spirit that impacts your life every day!

At elevateHim our heart is to promote, encourage and connect men and women to the freeing power of His grace and truth. Our greatest source for truth is the Word of God. While it is our life source, it can be overwhelming and intimidating to many. We labored with love and prayerfully created this resource to help all of us understand and embrace the authentic love-nature and sacrificial character of God.

We want to be a people, equipped by the Word, sharing the truth that also draws others into the Word. We never want to attract people to ourselves, to persuasive words or great books, but we want to draw people to the source of life and the One who loves them more than anyone else ever can. The Word of God is the greatest love story ever written.

We are here to support the shepherds who are equipping the sons and daughters with the Word and to be the church just as Christ commanded. As a team, we wrote this book together, not putting any one person's name on it. We proudly proclaim the good news of Jesus, the grace afforded us through the cross and the power of the Holy Spirit in our lives.

Whether you are a novice or an expert scholar we pray that the words in this book help you grow in the grace, love and power of the Holy Spirit.

With love,

The elevateHim Team

The Trinity

You can't earn God's love. You don't deserve God's love. He promised it through His Word. He chooses you because He loves you!

Week One - The Trinity

Day One - God the Father

God's Word is powerful. We have not just been called to read God's Word, but to study it. As we dive into His Word we will discover the true nature and character of God and the deep love-relationship He offers to His children. The elevateHim team desires that you not just read the Word but receive it as God speaking directly to you.

God is the Father of all Creation

Let's start at the very beginning. Grab your Bible and read Genesis Chapters 1-2.

How exactly did God create the heavens and the earth? This subject has been debated throughout human history. Almost every ancient religion has its own story to explain creation, and almost every scientist has an opinion on the origin of the Universe. However, the Bible is the only source that shows one supreme God creating the earth out of His great love and giving all people a specific and special purpose in it.

According to Genesis 1:3, 1:6, 1:9, 1:14, 1:20, and 1:24, how did God create the heavens and the earth? _____

In just a few verses, we discover that when God speaks and commands something out of nothing, it appears. Everything that has been created was created by God's voice. There is no God like the God of the Bible. Our God and Father is set far above every other mythical and false god. We will also discover that God not only created the heavens and the earth, but mankind as well. Let's look at this next Bible verse together so we can uncover how God the Father, the Son and the Holy Spirit created human beings.

God is Three in One

*Then God said, "**Let us** make human beings in **our image**, to be like* *ourselves. They will reign over the fish of the sea, the birds of the sky, the livestock, all the wild animals on the earth, and the small animals that scurry along the ground." So, God created human beings in His own image. In the image of God, He created them; male and female He created them. Then God blessed them and said, "Be fruitful and multiply. Fill the earth and govern it. Reign over the birds of the sky, and all the animals that scurry along the ground"* (Genesis 1:26-28 NLT).

There are two unique revelations in this passage. First, God is not alone in His creating, and second, we were created in the image of the Trinity.

God the Father is one part of the Trinity. That's an incredible revelation for us to believe and receive. Right here, ("**Let us make human beings in our image**") in the genesis of our creation, God (the Father) speaks to Jesus (the Son) and the Holy Spirit! Not only does God the Father speak to create, but the Holy Trinity (**God the Father, the Son and the Holy Spirit**) communicate with each other in unity and harmony in the creation of mankind. You are the image bearer of God!

Being made in the image of the Father, Son and Holy Spirit means that our spirit, soul and body, reflects the very image of the Trinity. Therefore, you were created perfectly in God's image. You have His DNA smeared throughout your entire being. God's nature and character is reflected in our unique design and creation. God loved us so much that He created us in the image of the Trinity. No other star, plant, animal, or creation possess this unique quality of being made in His image.

God Speaks Blessings Over You

Take a look at Genesis 1:28 and see if you can discover what He spoke over you. We see over and over that God's voice is powerful. God uses His voice to bless His children. Many people can receive that God spoke the heavens and earth into existence, yet they struggle to believe that God would use His voice to speak a blessing over them personally.

He blessed and empowered you to be fruitful and multiply in all you do. Every person on the planet needs the blessing of a Father. You might not have a good earthly father but today we see that God the Father blesses you and desires that you prosper in this life! Do you understand that God not only created you, but He also chose you?

God Chose You

*The Lord did not set His affection on you and **choose you**, because you were more numerous than other peoples, for you were the fewest of all peoples. But it was because **the Lord loved you** and kept the oath he swore to your ancestors that he brought you out with a mighty hand and redeemed you from the land of slavery, from the power of Pharaoh King of Egypt (Deuteronomy 7:7-8 NIV).*

As it was with the chosen people, Israel, so it is with us. God chooses us because He loves us and not because of any special virtue in us. God's nature is 100% pure love! He chose you not because you are strong or able to pay Him back but rather because He desires to walk in relationship with you. God doesn't want to be a part of your life…He wants to BE your life! You can't earn God's love. You don't deserve God's love. He promised it through His Word. **You are chosen because He loves you.**

We were created in the image of ___The trinity___

What are the 3 basic names of the Trinity?

1. ___The Father___   2. ___The Son___   3. ___Holy Spirit___

After today's Bible study, here's what we can see about God's nature:

- God has the power to create with His voice
- I was created by the Father, Son and Holy Spirit
- God loved me so much that He created me in His image
- God chose me

Every week we will focus on a verse for you to memorize so you can have God's Word hidden in your heart. Your verse for this week:

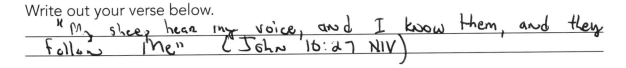

"My sheep hear My voice, and I know them, and they follow Me" (John 10:27 NIV).

Write out your verse below.

___"My sheep hear my voice, and I know them, and they follow Me" (John 10:27 NIV)___

Week One - The Trinity

Day Two - The Sin that Separates

Yesterday we talked about the nature of God. His voice spoke the earth into existence and you were created in the image of the Father, Son and Holy Spirit. The story of creation is beautiful, but the mind-blowing part, three chapters into Genesis the war begins. Sin enters the world and becomes our new reality.

It seems overwhelming to tackle all the issues of sin and how it landed in the hearts of men and women. In an effort to shorten an even longer narrative, the Word of God tells the story plain enough for all to understand where and how sin began.

Sin and the Curse

Grab your Bible and take time to read Genesis 3:1-24. As you read, think through these questions: How did the enemy twist the truth? Who did they choose to listen to? Make sure and write down some of your thoughts as you're reading.

He said that God didn't really intend for them not to
cut from it. Chose to listen to the serpent

Why was the tree forbidden ?

Quickly, we see that Adam and Eve were tempted and partnered with the devil, disguised as a serpent. Adam and Eve chose to believe satan; they defied God's protection and authority by taking God's place (of knowing good and evil) and decided for themselves what was best for their lives. Sin always separates.

Now, read Genesis 2:15 underlining what man was put in the garden to do.

The Lord God took the man [He had made] and settled him in the

*Garden of Eden to cultivate and keep it. And the Lord God command-
ed the man, saying, "You may freely (unconditionally) eat [the fruit]
from every tree of the garden; but [only] from the tree of the knowledge (recognition) of good and evil you shall not eat, otherwise on the
day that you eat from it, you shall most certainly die [because of your
disobedience]." (Genesis 2:15-17 AMP).*

God clearly gave Adam instructions. Now, let's read the passage that follows a few verses later. The serpent perverted the simplicity man was created to cultivate and introduced his destructive lies.

*"You will not certainly die," the serpent said to the woman. "For God
knows that when you eat from it your eyes will be opened, and you
will be like God, knowing good and evil" (Genesis 3:4-5 NIV).*

According to this passage, what did Eve think she would gain? _Recognition of knowledge_

When Adam and Eve tasted the fruit, they allowed the seed of the enemy (pride) to defile their identity. Adam and Eve took the fruit, which represented sin, and allowed themselves to be deceived by the enemy, so that they could be like God (knowing good and evil). According to the passage, the fruit looked pleasing for gaining wisdom, yet the curse of knowing this was more destructive than they realized.   _What is my identity_

The simple act of disobedience by Adam and Eve RELINQUISHED all mankind's power, perfection and right-standing with God. Their willful sin opened the legal floodgate for the enemy to unleash death and destruction on mankind. Immedi-
ately, we see that shame, fear, blame, and guilt were the fruit of their unwillingness to yield to God's instructions. The enemy will always try to convince you that God is holding you back and deceitfully encourage you to step where you have clearly been instructed not to go. From this day on, mankind was infected with the curse that they could not possibly rid themselves of or pay for.

The Bigger Plan

God set boundaries for Adam and Eve. Satan schemed to take God's place and bring disunity and animosity between the Creator and His creation. If this story were to stop here, it would be tragic at best. However, a clue of God's plan is found in the following scripture:

And I will put enmity between you and the woman, And between your seed and her seed; He shall bruise you on the head, And you shall bruise him on the heel (Genesis 3:15 KJV).

Satan believed he had dealt the death blow to God's plan for family and the atmosphere of unity and peace. The devil had successfully crafted a deceitful lie, and the children of God gobbled it up like little kids in a candy store. **Adam and Eve chose to believe a lie from the serpent over the words of their loving Father who created them.**

Every day we are faced with the same choices Adam and Eve encountered: either trust the voice and truth of God or partner with the lies of the enemy that disrupt our unity with God and each other. The enemy's plan is always to distract and destroy us with his lies, but the Father's plan is always love, grace, truth, and a future full of hope and purpose.

God offers truth and the enemy offers lies. Sin separates when we choose the lies of the enemy as our source instead of the Truth. It becomes very clear that two opposing powers want us, but only one loves us. In a recent Bible study a wonderful thought was introduced. What if Eve's response to the enemy was to pause and go to the Father instead of responding immediately to the enemy? Or, what if man had stopped his wife and recommended that they go together to their Father? Oh, how things could have been different.

A lie is anything that stands against the truth in God's Word and doesn't line up with the nature and character of God. When we choose to partner with a lie it kills marriages, relationships and brings spiritual chaos into our lives.

The Word gives life and the ability to identify anything that is counterfeit. We can learn from Adam and Eve and start today bringing every lie before our Creator and searching for the truth.

As we were sitting here writing this as a team we realized we can often assume that people can identify truth from lies. As we learn to study His Word, we discover that He is the only one who truly loves us. The reason we are studying God's Word and hiding the Word of God in our hearts is so that we can recognize God's love. God sets boundaries out of love, not to restrict our joy. God's nature is to provide, protect and heal.

When sin entered into the world, through the enemy's lies, the purpose was to separate us from God; from His love, His presence and His truth.

When lies come at you, do you have a tendency to marinate on the lies or search for the truth?

Without question's I can easily get wrapped up in the chaos that it brings.

What lie from the enemy have you believed more than the truth from God?

That im alone, inadequate, not enough or that i would not be missed if gone

I struggle alot witho the lie that I don't have fulfilling relationships whether friendship or intimate

What is the truth from God that needs to replace the lie from the enemy?

That I'm loved by God and others and he has a plan

Remember our verse for this week? Can you see the value of hiding this week's verse in your heart?

> *"My sheep hear My voice, and I know them, and they follow Me"* (John 10:27 NIV).

The Word gives life!

Week One - The Trinity

Day Three - Jesus the Son

Today we are going to tackle the nature and character of Jesus in relationship to us. Sometimes we overlook the depth of love and sacrifice God gave us through His son Jesus.

Jesus is the Word

God's only begotten Son came into this world to express His great love for His sons and daughters.

God's divine purpose was prearranged around Jesus Christ. When Jesus was born, we see that God was purposeful from the beginning. His plan was always for Jesus to dwell among us in the flesh. God's humility and love were on display for all mankind. He loved us so much that He was willing to put on the same dirt suit (flesh) we wear and overcome sin while wearing it!

> *The Word became flesh and made his dwelling among us. We have seen his glory, the glory of the one and only Son, who came from the Father, full of grace and truth* (John 1:14 NIV).

Jesus Christ, the "Word", was born, fully God and fully man in the flesh. He was tempted by sin like all people, yet unlike all other humans, He had the power to resist any and all temptation of the flesh. Jesus lived a perfect life in harmony with His Father. Here is the massive truth we must believe and receive: Jesus is the only man who has lived or ever will live a perfect, faultless life. *He committed no sin and no deceit was found in his mouth* (1 Peter 2:22 NIV).

Yesterday you read about how sin entered through man. Many people become confused about the topic of sin and the need for a savior. Couldn't God just forgive Adam and Eve and put things back in order? God is a righteous judge and will not bend His nature and character to conform with man. Their sin had real and deadly consequences as a result of their choices.

Jesus is the Lamb that was Slain

However, we are not left without hope. Because God is all-knowing, He ordained Jesus to come as a sin offering before He ever created the world. John 1:29 says that Jesus Christ is the Lamb of God who died for the sins of the world. His mission and purpose became clear to mankind only after He had been crucified on the cross.

Peter echoes this truth in even more detail when he writes about the precious blood of Jesus Christ.

> For you know that it was not with perishable things such as silver or gold that you were redeemed from the empty way of life handed down to you from your forefathers, but with the precious blood of Christ, a lamb without blemish or defect. **He was chosen before the creation of the world, but was revealed in these last times for your sake** (1 Peter 1:18-20 NIV).

What a game changer when we discover God's relentless love for us, His display of being the all-knowing God, and the blood of Jesus demolished satan's hold on mankind!

Do you see the goodness of God? God in His foreknowledge knew that Jesus would give His life, but this truth was hidden from satan. Before the creation of the world, God knew. Yet no one on earth, not even satan, knew about the shed blood until Jesus' death, burial, and resurrection. This truth, once we understand it, should have great implications for our faith and victorious living over satan and sin.

Jesus is the Life-Giving Gift

We love the Message version of Romans 5:15-19. Here we see that Jesus is the final solution to sin and our need for reconciliation to God. Take a minute and read through these verses below.

> Yet the rescuing gift is not exactly parallel to the death-dealing sin. If one man's sin put crowds of people at the dead-end abyss of separation from God, just think what God's gift poured through one man, Jesus Christ, will do! There's no comparison between that death-dealing sin and this generous, life-giving gift. The verdict on that one sin

was the death sentence; the verdict on the many sins that followed was this wonderful life sentence. If death got the upper hand through one man's wrongdoing, can you imagine the breathtaking recovery life makes, sovereign life, in those who grasp with both hands this wildly extravagant life-gift, this grand setting-everything-right, that the one-man Jesus Christ provides? Here it is in a nutshell: Just as one person did it wrong and got us in all this trouble with sin and death, another person did it right and got us out of it. But more than just getting us out of trouble, he got us into life! One man said no to God and put many people in the wrong; one man said yes to God and put many in the right (Romans 5:15-19 MSG).

We have a choice every day to say yes or no to God. Every time we say yes, we are embracing THE LIFE-GIVING gift of Jesus.

When sin entered the world, we needed someone to rescue us.

The enemy tried to deceive and bring down mankind. God had an ace in the hole; Jesus! Today, we want to introduce you to Jesus, the son of God, Jesus the Word, and Jesus the lamb that was slain. The more intimately we get to know God through the Word the more intimately we know Jesus. Jesus' nature and character is laced and traced with sacrifice, love, grace, and truth.

Have you accepted Jesus as your LIFE-GIVING gift? ___Yes___

Does the life and death of Jesus have an impact on your daily life? Why or why not?
___Yes, but I yearn for it to have a greater___
___impact___

In your own words write out a prayer telling Jesus who He is to you and thanking Him for what He has done and is doing for you.
___Dear Father, how I love you and the precious gift___
___of your Son you to gave to me. I will continue___
___to live each day for you & to make you proud___
___Amen___

Week One - The Trinity

Day Four - Holy Spirit is the Ultimate Gift-Giver

It may seem strange for me to say, "I would like to present to you the Holy Spirit." Many might see the Holy Spirit as an abstract thought or even a kooky-spooky thing that only ultra-charismatic circles use. Who is the Holy Spirit? To many the Holy Spirit is nothing more than a powerless part of the Trinity, or a very religious reference used by priests, preachers and clergy. Others have limited the Holy Spirit to the gifts of tongues and prophecies, but He is so much more. **The Holy Spirit empowers us and gives us much more than the gifts; He offers us relationship.**

The Holy Spirit is the 3rd person in the Trinity, and He not only has a name, but He has an active daily role in believers' lives. He doesn't have a physical body nor a face we can recognize, yet His personality is laced with love, comfort and power that is undeniable.

What is your definition of the Holy Spirit? Please share why you believe what you believe.

That feeling you get, sorta a feeling of something coming over you when you think, worship or pray to God

Did you know that the very nature of God the Father, God the Son and God the Holy Spirit is that they are all givers?

- God the Father gave His only begotten Son.
- The Son gave the Holy Spirit to those who believe in the Son.
- The Holy Spirit is a wise counselor and gives gifts to men and women to operate in supernatural power as ambassadors of truth.

Read what Jesus says in John 16 about the Holy Spirit.

"But very truly I tell you, it is for your good that I am going away. Unless I go away, the Advocate will not come to you; but if I go, I will *send him to you. When he comes, he will prove the world to be in the wrong about sin and righteousness and judgment: about sin, because people do not believe in me; about righteousness, because I am going to the Father, where you can see me no longer; and about judgment, because the prince of this world now stands condemned. I have much more to say to you, more than you can now bear. But when he, the Spirit of truth, comes, he will guide you into all the truth. He will not speak on his own; he will speak only what he hears, and he will tell you what is yet to come. He will glorify me because it is from me that he will receive what he will make known to you. All that belongs to the Father is mine. That is why I said the Spirit will receive from me what he will make known to you"* (John 16:7-15 NIV).

When Jesus ascended to the right hand of the Father, He sent the Holy Spirit to reveal to us the truth about Himself, the truth about our own lives and to equip us for ministry.

The Holy Spirit is our Counselor

The Greek word used for the Holy Spirit is *'Parakletos'* and is translated as counselor. This literally means "someone called to one's side", and sometimes this is translated as "advocate, comforter, intercessor, or consoler". The Holy Spirit, for us as believers, is the One who guides us into all truth and comforts us. He comforts us about the true identity of Jesus as the Christ, and our true identity as sons and daughters of God.

The Holy Spirit Gives Gifts for the Body

Each person has been given unique gifts to be used in the body of Christ.

> *There are different kinds of gifts, but the same Spirit distributes them. There are different kinds of service, but the same Lord. There are different kinds of working, but in all of them and in everyone it is the same God at work. Now to each one the manifestation of the Spirit is given for the common good. To one there is given through the Spirit a message of wisdom, to another a message of knowledge by means of the same Spirit, to another faith by the same Spirit, to another gifts of healing by that one Spirit, to another miraculous powers, to another prophecy, to another distinguishing between spirits, to another speaking in different kinds of tongues, and to still another the interpretation of tongues. All these are the work of one and the same Spirit, and*

he distributes them to each one, just as he determines (1 Corinthians 12:4-11 NIV).

Yes, there are many gifts He desires to give. We must all be led by Him to use these gifts to demonstrate the love of Christ, first to other believers in our family and second, to a lost and dying world. We are the body of Christ and all have a special and specific destiny to play in the expression of God's love to this world. You were uniquely made by the Father, the Son and the Holy Spirit as a one of a kind work of art. The Holy Spirit desires to have relationship not only for your benefit, but for the benefit of the entire Kingdom of God.

The Holy Spirit Comes Through Relationship

Dear brothers and sisters, we need to learn to develop our relationship with the One who guides us into all truth. If He is received by the grace and truth by which He is given, He will POUR HIMSELF in and through us.

How would you describe your relationship with the Holy Spirit?

Just getting started. I'm still learning to decipher when/ how/ why the Holy Spirit is in me.

The Word describes the Holy Spirit as our advocate, support, protection, strength, guidance, and companion. He is all these things and more, but which one of these specifically do you need Him to be for you today? Spend time in prayer today telling Holy Spirit what you need from Him. He is waiting for us to share our hearts and needs with Him and loves our honesty and vulnerability.

Support / Protection / Guidance / Companion

Week One - The Trinity

Day Five - Open the Gift

One of my favorite things to do is give gifts. As a matter of fact, I look for opportunities to give my time, talents, treasures, touch and words away to people.

I remember one particular evening when I was at a gas station filling up after a long day. I watched a man drive up to the gas pump just behind me. As soon as he drove up I felt compassion, joy, and the gift of giving bubbling up inside of me. I ran over to his pump with credit card in hand and inserted my card. He quickly jumped out of his car and responded with, "Hey mister, this is my pump!" I replied, "I know, and I want to pay for your gas. As a matter of fact, I just did, so fill up!" As I walked back over to my truck, I glanced over my shoulder to see what he was doing. He just stood there with a confused face while I watched his emotions change from feelings of frustration to shock. After inserting the gas nozzle into his tank, he walked slowly over to me. He asked me if I was a believer. I replied with a big smile, "Yes sir, I am." He then explained that he was a drummer on the worship team at a local church. He was on his way to church and had just told the Lord he didn't know how he was going to have enough gas money for the week. God allowed me to use my gifts to bless someone else.

Giving and Receiving Gifts

Do you like to give or receive gifts? Explain why or why not.

Yes I love to give's Mostly my time but sometimes money I'm sure I like to receive although it doesn't happen often

We all have reasons why we like or dislike to give or receive. The team at elevate-Him Ministries is passionate about helping you and other brothers and sisters grow in the Word, wisdom and power of God's grace and truth. I want to be a good spiritual member of God's household. One of the greatest ways to grow in your relationship with God is by receiving what He has freely given to you. As a wise man said, "You can't give away what you don't have". So the question is: have you received all God has for you?

Story Time:

Once upon a time, there was a little girl named Joy who received a gift at Christmas. The present was very big and wrapped perfectly, just waiting for Joy to come snatch it up from under the Christmas tree. Joy walked slowly and cautiously to the present not wanting to be disappointed. She thought, "Surely this large of a gift couldn't be for me!" Her feet finally shuffled next to the present. Her head shifted down while her eyes read...

To: Joy

From: Father, Son and Holy Spirit

She picked up the present with great delight, dancing around the house with it singing. She carried the gift for hours, days, and shockingly years having never opened the gift.

I know this story sounds absurd, but it happens every day. In the story about Joy, it seems she receives the gift, but in all actuality, she just picks it up, never opening it. There is a big difference between holding a gift in your hands and opening it to reveal what has been given to you.

Unwrapping our Gift

There are many believers who have been given the gift of the Holy Spirit but have yet to open and receive it. My desire is over the next few weeks you begin to open the gifts that have been wrapped and given just for you! The Father is a precious, loving and unshakable gift. He desires a unique relationship with you!

The Son, Jesus, was given as a gift, but many choose not to receive Him for a variety of misguided reasons. If you have never received the gift of Jesus, maybe today is the day. You can accept the gift and receive Him in your heart. (To learn more about this go to page 177).

Last but not least, the sweet Holy Spirit continues to be the gift that is held the most but never opened. We have listened to the stories of what He looks and acts like, but like small, frightened children, we are too scared to see for ourselves what is in the box.

It is time for you to have a relationship with all three: the Father, the Son and the

Holy Spirit. They all desire a personal relationship with you and can't wait for you to open the gifts they have waiting for you!

Check out these verses below.

> *Every good gift and every perfect gift is from above, coming down from the **Father** of lights with whom there is no variation or shadow due to change* (James 1:17 ESV).

> *But the gift is not like the trespass. For if the many died by the trespass of the one man, how much more did God's grace and the gift that came by the grace of the one man, **Jesus Christ**, abound to the many* (Romans 5:15 NIV).

> *"So I say to you: Ask and it will be given to you; seek and you will find; knock and the door will be opened to you. For everyone who asks receives; the one who seeks finds; and to the one who knocks, the door will be opened. Which of you fathers, if your son asks for a fish, will give him a snake instead? Or if he asks for an egg, will give him a scorpion? If you then, though you are evil, know how to give good gifts to your children, how much more will your Father in heaven give the **Holy Spirit** to those who ask him"* (Luke 11:9-13 NIV).

Have you opened the gifts that you've been given? _Not all but I'm getting there_

If not, what's holding you back?
Fear

If you are ready, let's pray this prayer together:

Lord, I want to fully embrace and enjoy the gift of God, Jesus and the Holy Spirit. Today I choose to receive the Holy Spirit as my counselor, companion and friend. I want to walk in the power of the Holy Spirit and the gifts of the Holy Spirit. I invite you to fill me, so I can overflow with your gifts to the church and a lost and dying world.

Tomorrow is a special day; at the end of each week we will have a special devotion on rest and what it means to lean on the Lord.

Week One - The Trinity

Day Six - The Purpose of Rest

By the seventh day God had finished the work He had been doing; so on the seventh day He rested from all of His work. Then God blessed the seventh day and made it holy, because on it He rested from all the work of creating that He had done (Genesis 2:2-3 NIV).

God set into motion the pattern of work and rest. In the beginning, as God created, He knew that His work was good, so He rested on the seventh day. Jesus, in the middle of His ministry, often took time away to rest and pray.

He created us for His purpose and part of that purpose is rest. Many times, we can have the wrong idea about what rest is and what rest isn't. For the hard-working performer, rest can feel like failure. For the multi-tasking, super-driven business owner, rest can seem lazy. For the busy mom of four, running the minivan taxi service, rest can feel like an impossibility.

The sweet truth from our loving Father is that He desires to meet us in our rest. Yes, He meets us in our going and doing, our seeking and serving, but He longs for us to just be still. **Rest, by definition, is ceasing work or movement for the purpose of refreshing oneself and recovering strength.** The Lord's will is for us to be able to rest in Him in any and every situation.

He says, "Be still, and know that I am God; I will be exalted among the nations, I will be exalted in the earth" (Psalm 46:10 NIV).

We can rest in the Holy Community of the Father, Son and Holy Spirit. They are one, and we get to benefit from their oneness! The Father created us to rest. Jesus died so that we could have the ultimate rest in our eternal security, and the Holy Spirit ministers to us as we rest.

Read through these scriptures about rest and make note of what stands out to you.

Come to me, all you who are weary and burdened, and I will give you rest. Take my yoke upon you and learn from me, for I am gentle and humble in heart, and you will find rest for your souls. For my yoke is easy and my burden is light (Matthew 11:28-30 NIV).

So then, there remains a Sabbath rest for the people of God (Hebrews 4:9 ESV).

Let us therefore strive to enter that rest, so that no one may fall by the same sort of disobedience (Hebrews 4:11 ESV).

When we get tired, worn out and burned out, it's a sure sign that there's something missing. We look to everything and everyone to fill the void that can only be filled by Him. It's in the place of rest where we are refreshed, refilled and refueled, so we can walk in step with our Creator who loves us and has BIG plans for us!

Take a few minutes today and jot down your personal definition of rest.

_____

_____

_____

_____

Now take that to the Father in prayer asking Him to show you what real rest in Him looks like for you. What do you need from Him as you rest? Write down what the Father says to you about this.

_____

_____

_____

_____

Will you make a commitment to rest today? If so, share that with Him through prayer.

Faith by Grace

Grace makes a new way, His way, not only possible but completely achievable.

Week Two - Faith by Grace

Day One - Grace is the Lens of Love

As we start to unpack the gospel of grace, we must begin with one important concept: **God offers His love to everyone**. Let me encourage you to put on the lens of love. Without love, it isn't beneficial to read any of this. As we go through this week, we will explore and understand the love nature of God embodied in grace. We want to recognize grace and see it in action in our everyday lives. Because of God's great love, grace is available to us.

Have you ever worn sunglasses with colored lenses? When you're wearing colored lenses, everything you see through those lenses will look slightly tinted. If they're rose colored, everything you see looks pink. Those fun mirrored glasses make everything look blue. In our lives, the lens we are looking through tints every thought, word and action. When we put on the lens of love, we begin to hear, see and experience God's nature and character undefiled, regardless of our weaknesses.

Does that surprise you? Have you held any belief that because of sin, God only loves those who are perfect, don't sin, strive for perfection and walk in obedience?

God Loves without Condition

The truth is, we all fall short (Romans 3:23).

Do you believe God loves everyone? _Yes_

Do you believe God loves you? _Of course_

> *For God so loved the world that he gave his only begotten Son, that whosoever believes in Him shall not perish, but have eternal life (John 3:16 KJV).*

Although you've likely heard this verse before, what have you believed about any conditions concerning God's love?

That I must be perfect

When we talk about God's love, we need to understand love in the context of how the word is used in the New Testament. There are various types of love mentioned in the New Testament, and today we are going to focus on two: *agape* and *phileo*. *Agape* is an unconditional, sacrificial, selfless love. It is the feeling or emotion of the preciousness of the object; whereas *phileo* love is a brotherly, or relational, type of love. It's a sense of delight found in the object that is loved. God loves everyone *(agape)*, but He has a relational love *(phileo)* for those who have received His Son and love Him. God loves *(agape)* you. There's nothing you can do to keep Him from loving *(agape)* you. Even if you choose to reject His love, it is still available to you. When you choose to believe in Jesus and receive His love *(agape)* for you, He now has a new love *(phileo)* relationship with you that becomes intimate and personal.

Saved by Grace

If God loves everyone, why does He allow some to be cast into hell and spend eternity apart from Him? Remember, God loves everyone, and He chose us, but we must respond to His love and choose Him. You do not go to heaven because God loves you, but because you receive Him as the Lord and Savior of your life. You don't spend eternity with God because you alter your behavior or spend your time caring for others. You receive eternal life in heaven by confessing with your mouth and believing in your heart that Jesus is Lord. Read Romans 10:9 and Ephesians 2:8-9.

> If you declare with your mouth "Jesus is Lord" and believe in your heart that God raised him from the dead, you will be saved (Romans 10:9 NIV).

> For it is by grace you have been saved, through faith—and this is not from yourselves, it is the gift of God—not by works, so that no one can boast (Ephesians 2:8-9 NIV).

Salvation is a gift of grace. We don't deserve it, but God's Word promises it to those who believe.

Explain below in your own words how we are saved.

We are saved by God's Grace. He gave up his Son to show his love for us

Now look at this scripture in Peter.

> *The Lord is not slow in keeping his promise, as some understand slowness. Instead he is patient with you, not wanting anyone to perish, but everyone to come to repentance (2 Peter 3:9 NIV).*

According to the Word, God reaches out to all of His children with the hope that they will choose to turn to Him and embrace His love instead of darkness. His desire is for us all to come to repentance. He loves us and waits patiently for us.

Grace is the basis for everything we believe and receive in the Christian faith because without grace, we would be eternally separated from God as a result of our own imperfections.

Do you feel like you personally know or understand grace? In your own words, describe what God's grace means to you.

This week's verse we will memorize together is Romans 11:16. We love the ESV version, but you are welcome to use any translation you'd like. It's always a good practice to read a scripture in various versions and find the one that you connect with best.

> *But if it is by grace you have been saved, it is no longer on the basis of works; otherwise grace would no longer be grace (Romans 11:6 ESV).*

Write this scripture out on a post-it note or note card and keep it with you all week. Read it out loud throughout your day and share it every chance you get. Grace is an incredible gift we've been given. Let's live in grace together today and every day!

Week Two - Faith by Grace

Day Two - Grace and Faith Work

Yesterday we asked you to put on the lens of love. With that lens, let's dive into the concept of grace.

> *For it is by grace you have been saved, through faith—and this is not from yourselves, it is the gift of God— not by works, so that no one can boast* (Ephesians 2:8-9 NIV).

The word grace in Greek is *charis* and means merciful kindness. This is the kindness God uses to call us to Himself and bring others to Him.

Grace Came Through Jesus

The truth and grace that we find in the New Testament is a beautiful picture of Jesus Christ Himself. We are no longer judged on our merits, works or shortcomings, but we have been forever cleansed by the blood of Jesus and right-standing with our Father. The Lamb of God (John 1:29) truly shed His blood, and the Father looks through the lens of Jesus and sees you as perfect. Words that describe grace are joy, favor, delight, sweetness, loveliness and pleasure. **Grace isn't accomplished or earned by the works of man. It's not about what we do but what He did.**

The law came from God through Moses. Grace and truth came through Jesus and is guarded by the Holy Spirit.

Read John 1:17.

> *For the Law was given through Moses, but grace [the unearned, undeserved favor of God] and truth came through Jesus Christ* (John 1:17 AMP).

For our definition today: **Grace is unmerited favor and supernatural power that allows us to accomplish the will of God!**

Where have you seen **God's unmerited favor** or **supernatural power** in your life?

His help in helping to abstain from drinking.

The concept of grace is not just New Testament theology. In the purest sense of the word, grace is receiving something we don't deserve. It's seen as early as Genesis 15:6.

> And Abram believed the LORD, and the LORD counted him as righteous because of his faith (Genesis 15:6 NLT).

Righteousness is not based on us, but on the One who loves us.

Faith and Grace

Abram believed God and trusted the nature and character of God. It was through Abram's faith alone that he was declared righteous before the Lord. What's important about this moment is that Abram had not done anything to qualify himself for the love of God. He was declared righteous _before_ he was set aside and circumcised; _before_ he negotiated with God about the destruction of Sodom; _before_ God changed his name to Abraham; and _before_ his son Isaac was born. This is what Paul is talking about in the book of Romans. As Paul lays out his message of grace, he starts with the fact that Abraham himself received the gift of righteousness through faith alone.

Abram and Abraham are the same person. God changed his name when He gave him a promise.

> What then shall we say was gained by Abraham, our forefather according to the flesh? For if Abraham was justified by works, he has something to boast about, but not before God. For what does the Scripture say? 'Abraham believed God, and it was counted to him as righteousness.' Now to the one who works, his wages are not counted as a gift but as his due. And to the one who does not work but believes in him who justifies the ungodly, his faith is counted as righteousness (Romans 4:1-5 ESV).

Paul then goes on to explain that just as Abraham had received justification through faith, we also have the same opportunity through faith in Jesus Christ. The promise to

Abraham is a foretelling of the grace that is coming to the Gentiles (a Gentile is anyone who is not Jewish).

> *Therefore, since we have been justified by faith, we have peace with God through our Lord Jesus Christ. Through him we have also obtained access by faith into this grace in which we stand, and we rejoice in hope of the glory of God* (Romans 5:1-2 ESV).

Grace and faith work. We don't have to work for the free gift of God (salvation). We've been called to simply believe. By faith we can live in grace.

Where in your life have you been working to receive God's love and grace?

Marriage - My desire to marry a woman of God

What sin have you struggled with that the enemy uses to try and tell you that you are disqualified from the love of God? Journal your thoughts below:

Feeling of past sins + guilt

Freedom comes when we choose not to focus on our sin but rather on the love of God that sets us free. Freedom is not the absence of sin in our life but the life-giving presence of Jesus.

Week Two - Faith by Grace

Day Three - Grace Not by Works

Yesterday we talked about Abraham and how he believed God, and it was credited to him as righteousness. He was given a promise but also a warning about what would happen when his people rebelled. God delivers the law to Moses 430 years later. Once the law was given to the Israelites on Mt. Sinai, their justification was now based on a small list of commandments and several complex rules and regulations that they must follow (you can read through this story in Exodus 19-20). What they thought would be a simple way to obey the Lord was impossible to fulfill.

The Israelites at Mt. Sinai responded in arrogance truly thinking they could do what God was saying in their own strength. **The law was never intended to make us perfect but to draw us to the perfect One.** God was not setting us up for failure (because He knew the impossibility of following the letter of the Law). The Law was setting us up for relationship with Him!

Read Galatians 2:21.

> *I do not set aside the grace of God, for if righteousness could be gained through the law, Christ died for nothing* (Galatians 2:21 NIV).

According to the above verse, trying to gain righteousness by obeying the law is setting aside grace. Paul is very clear that anytime you try to achieve right standing with God by your own works, you are actually rejecting God and nullifying the redeeming work of Jesus on the cross. BAM ♥!

Grace through Jesus

Read through Galatians 3:23-29.

> *Now before faith came, we were held captive under the law, imprisoned*

until the coming faith would be revealed. So then, the law was our guardian until Christ came, in order that we might be justified by faith. But now that faith has come, we are no longer under a guardian, for in Christ Jesus you are all sons of God, through faith. For as many of you as were baptized into Christ have put on Christ. There is neither Jew nor Greek, there is neither slave nor free, there is no male and female, for you are all one in Christ Jesus. And if you are Christ's, then you are Abraham's offspring, heirs according to promise (Galatians 3:23-29 MSG).

In day 2, we talked about Jesus and how He is described as grace, peace and truth. We love The Message version above because many times we view the law though a negative lens. We can live our lives trying to measure up or by holding a measuring stick to others in accordance with the law, instead of offering what was freely given to us. The law was our guardian to lead us and protect us until the coming of Jesus. We have been given the unmerited favor of grace, mercy, and truth in the person of Jesus.

Do you have a tendency to keep records of your wrongs? _No -Sometimes_

Do you have a tendency to keep records of the wrongs of others? _Sometimes_

Read 1 Corinthians 13 in your Bible. According to the end of verse 5, what does Paul say about keeping record of wrongs? _____

Does this change in any way how you now look at the law and how you have tried to achieve God's favor through your own actions? Take a few minutes and write your response below.
To have a greater focus on Relationship instead of merely by acts or works (IE following laws)

Redeemed from the Law

Now read through Galatians chapter 3.

According to Paul's writings in Galations 3:10 (CSV), Paul makes an incredibly bold statement when he said *"For all who rely on the works of the law are under a curse, because it is written, Everyone who does not do everything written in the book of the law is cursed."*

Read the passage below in James.

> *For whoever keeps the whole law and yet stumbles at just one point is guilty of breaking all of it* (James 2:10 NIV).

You can't pick and choose which points of the law to attempt to obey and then also claim to be righteous through grace. As James explains, failing in one makes you guilty of them all. You are either saved by grace, or you are judged by the law (Romans 2:12).

Are there certain parts of the law that you have tried to maintain for any reason? Share below those times and reject the lies of the enemy that have enslaved you in the past.

Lust being less of a Sin than others so it is
okay to committ.

> *But if it is by grace, then it is no longer on the basis of works; otherwise grace would no longer be grace* (Romans 11:6 ESV).

God despises our sweat when it comes from trying to obtain His favor. Boasting in our works is a rejection of the gift of grace. When have you ever boasted in your works in order to try and achieve favor with God?

One of the best ways to apply scripture is writing His Word back to Him as a prayer. Using the scripture below, write a prayer to God thanking Him for His grace.

Thankful Lord, that you've blessed me beyond measur

> *For it is by grace you have been saved, through faith — and this is not from yourselves, it is the gift of God- not by works, so that no one can boast* (Ephesians 2:8-9 NIV).

Week Two - Faith by Grace

Day Four - Grace Over Judgment

You can rejoice in the fact that as a believer in Christ, you are no longer judged for your sin. Jesus made an exchange on the cross - His life for yours, His perfection for your imperfection, His holiness for your wickedness. You have been forgiven for your past, present and future sins. WHAT AN EXCHANGE! God now views you through the lens of His Perfect Son. He remembers your sins no longer.

> *And I will forgive their wickedness, and I will never again remember their sins* (Hebrews 8:12 NLT).

I once heard a pastor preach on this verse and he said, "The Bible does not say God forgets your sin…God is perfect, not forgetful. But…He CHOOSES to remember them no more. It's His CHOICE because of His love for you. What Jesus did on the cross allows Him to put aside your sins and not recognize them or even think on them ever again." This truth makes the scripture above even more powerful.

> *The LORD is compassionate and gracious, slow to anger, abounding in love. He will not always accuse, nor will he harbor his anger forever; he does not treat us as our sins deserve or repay us according to our iniquities. For as high as the heavens are above the earth, so great is his love for those who fear him; as far as the east is from the west, so far has he removed our transgressions from us* (Psalm 103:8-12 NIV).

How often have the sins of your past been brought to your own memory? How often have you thought about them and thrown yourself back in the abyss of pain and doubt? If God no longer remembers your sins, then who is it that is reminding you of them? As you process through these questions write your responses below.

Weekly

The enemy, as he wants me to wallow in them and fail

Pray and ask Holy Spirit to shine His light on the truth that covers the repetitive reminders of your past sins. Ask Him to highlight a scripture you can memorize that counteracts this tactic of the enemy.   Prov 4:23

Nothing is Hidden

> *There is nothing concealed that will not be disclosed, or hidden that will not be made known* (Luke 12:2 NIV).

In God's ability to be all-knowing and everywhere at the same time, nothing is hidden, and He is never surprised by our actions or any situation we will face. He knows what you have done, what you're doing, and what you will do, and He has declared you forgiven through the righteous blood of Jesus. He has declared you righteous, holy and perfect. Not through anything you have done but through the finished work of His Son on the cross. You are no longer under the curse of death but have been given the gift of eternal life!

> *Very truly I tell you, whoever hears my word and believes him who sent me has eternal life and **will not be judged** but has crossed over from death to life* (John 5:24 NIV).

Do you tend to judge yourself based on your failures? Do you discredit your salvation on the basis of your weaknesses? The scripture tells us we *will NOT be judged*. Are you ready to lay down your rights to self-condemnation and judgment based on your sin, actions and thoughts? Your seat at the table is given to you at salvation, and nothing you have done or will do can cause you to lose your place.

God isn't Disappointed in Us

Many believers have an image of God that is contradictory to the grace that Jesus provided. So many believe that whenever they sin, God is disappointed or angry at them. They believe that He distances Himself from them because of their sin, and that they must confess over and over again to be forgiven.

Where does this belief come from? Everyone has been rejected at some point. We have a tendency to put expectations on our heavenly Father based on the relationships modeled by parents and those in authority. But this view of God simply does not line up with His Word.

We do not confess our sins to be forgiven. We confess our sins because we are forgiven. **We come boldly before the throne of grace because the Father loves us,**

because Jesus gave us the gift of grace, and because the Holy Spirit leads us. The purpose of confession is to align our thoughts with the way God sees us. We will dig deeper into this in a few weeks.

Confession is a small part of living forgiven. Conviction many times is misinterpreted as condemnation… and that is not the heart or nature of our Creator. Right believing produces right behavior. Remember, everything is about the lens of grace, love and the Holy Spirit. It is the kindness of God that leads you to repentance (Romans 2:4).

Have you ever felt convicted or condemned because of your sin? Have you ever felt wrongly condemned or convicted? Describe below.

Both of these, I have felt conviction of my sins & also have been wrongly condemned, which is why I am no longer in the AF

Understand that God does not condemn you. If He did, then Romans 8:1 would not be true.

> Therefore, there is now no condemnation for those who are in Christ Jesus (Romans 8:1 NIV).

Grace Rescues us from Our Sin

God is passionate about you. He loves you. Ever since the fall of Adam, God's plan has been to rescue us from our sin. The entire ministry of Jesus was to illustrate God's love for us which climaxes at His ultimate sacrifice on the cross.

> For God was in Christ, reconciling the world to himself, no longer counting people's sins against them. And he gave us this wonderful message of reconciliation (2 Corinthians 5:19 NLT).

Have you believed that God is mad or disappointed in you or in anything you've done? ___Yes - 2017 liver___

Does God distance himself from you whenever you sin and wait for you to reconcile and come clean? Why not? Some say that because of grace, they are able to act and do whatever they please; through grace, they have been given a "get out of jail free" card, and their actions or works no longer matter. That's not only wrong thinking, but it is contrary to the truth in scripture. Jesus paid an expensive price for the gift of grace and believing that way would be cheapening the work of the cross.

The fact is that when we receive the amazing grace of God, we cannot help but respond with gratitude. James says, "Faith without works is dead." The shift between the old covenant of the law and the new covenant of grace doesn't mean that our actions do not matter anymore, it means that we are not saved by them. As a true believer, we cannot look at His sacrifice on the cross without being spurred on to show others the nature of Christ through our own lives.

We can strive and perform to prove something or modify our behavior based on how God has changed us. Are you motivated by a heart change because of grace, or works and performance? Take a minute and journal your response.

Motivated by heart change.
_____
_____
_____
_____
_____
_____
_____

Now, in light of everything we've studied this week, if someone were to ask you to describe God's grace, what would you say? Journal your thoughts as if you are sharing this amazing truth with a friend.

Grace is _____
_____
_____
_____
_____
_____
_____
_____
_____
_____

Grace Wins!

Week Two - Faith by Grace

Day Five - Grace Gives Identity

The gift of grace doesn't stop at God's forgiveness of our sins. He takes it even further by adopting you into the Royal Family and calling you a co-heir with Christ. Listen to how Paul builds this case of adoption:

> *All those led by God's Spirit are God's sons [and daughters]. For you did not receive a spirit of slavery to fall back into fear, but you received the Spirit of adoption, by whom we cry out, "Abba, Father!" The Spirit Himself testifies together with our spirit that we are God's children, and if children, also heirs — heirs of God and co-heirs with Christ… (Romans 8:15-17 ESV).*

He starts by saying that when Holy Spirit dwells in us, we are God's children (1 John 3:1). He also says we are heirs of God, brothers and sisters of Christ, and co-heirs with our brother Jesus. Why is this important to understand? Because this is our identity. When we believe this, we begin to fully grasp what it means to be a son or daughter of God (Galatians 3:26) and a co-heir with Christ.

The Assault on Our Identity

Satan knows this important fact, too. It is exactly why one of his most common tactics is to attack your identity. When the enemy can get you to believe that you are not who God says you are, then he has enslaved you into an orphan mentality and removed your power. You feel alone, unprotected, and without provision.

Take a moment and ask God who He says you are. Write His response here.
God says I am ___AMAZING___

What are some areas of your life that the enemy has convinced you that you're not who God says you are? (Ex: as a mom/dad, husband/wife, friend, coworker, leader, believer) *Alone + not able to be a husband*

How often do you see yourself through the lies of the enemy instead of the lens of God's love for you?
Days + weeks

One team member's response to this question as they were reading through this was honest and personal, and we wanted to share it with you. "I tend to see myself through the lies of the enemy instead of the lens of God's love too often and more than I care to admit. Sometimes it's momentary, other times I get stuck there for a day or two before I realize it and take authority over the lies". What about you, can you honestly respond to the question above?

It's easy, no matter where you are in your relationship with the Lord to get stuck in the lies, but His invitation is always there and He's waiting to tell us the TRUTH about who we are.

And here's the real truth… You are not stupid, alone, messed up, ugly, or rejected. In order to accept the truth of your identity, you must first walk in humility. Your greatest accomplishments are pale and insignificant in comparison to the accomplishments of Christ. Your identity is nothing that you can boast about through your own abilities. There is nothing you have done to deserve it. Through the finished work of the cross, you are adopted as a beloved child of God (John 1:12-13).

As Paul wrote in his letter to the Galatians, *But as for me, I will never boast about anything except the cross of our Lord Jesus Christ* (Galatians 6:14 NIV).

By walking in humility, you are drawing the attention away from yourself and allowing Christ to be glorified. Jesus is kind, strong, powerful, generous, full of love, compassionate, and so much more. Take a minute to write who you say Jesus is. How have you seen Him show up in your life? You can use some of the words above or write in your own.

Jesus is _____ *Powerful* _____

Jesus is _____ *Forgiving* _____

Jesus is ___full of Grace___

Jesus is ___close to God___

Do you realize that when God sees you, He sees Jesus?

> *By this is love perfected with us, so that we may have confidence for the day of judgment, because as he is so also are we in this world* (1 John 4:17 ESV).

John is writing about the fact that God sent His Son to this world as a settlement for our sin -- His greatest act of love! Through this act, His love is perfected in us, so that we may have confidence on the day of judgment that we are no longer judged. Why? Here is the amazing part…because as He is now, so are we in this world.

Think about this. It does not say "as He is, so we hope to be" or "as He is, so we try to be." It says we ARE. At this moment, you are everything Jesus is now. God views you through the perfection of your brother Jesus and has given you the same identity. Everything you wrote above about Jesus, He says YOU ARE, TOO!

See what great love the Father has lavished on us, that we should be called the children of God! And that is what we are! The reason the world does not know us is that it did not know Him

1 John 3:1 NIV

Week Two - Faith by Grace

Day Six - Resting in Grace

Remember grace is unmerited favor and the power to fulfill the will of God in our lives. Can you see that all the heavy lifting is in Jesus' hands not our human efforts? Our body and soul are naturally bent toward doing it on our own. **Grace makes a new way, His way, not only possible but completely achievable.**

> *Truly my soul finds rest in God; my salvation comes from him* (Psalm 62:1 NIV).

We are human. Divinely created and uniquely designed. We are made of three parts: body, soul and spirit. Our bodies are the dirt-suit we live in here on earth. Our spirits were placed inside of us, and it's where we commune with God. Our soul is our mind, will and emotions. Our soul is where we think, feel and make decisions. As the Trinity is three parts, so are we because we are made in His image.

Where do you see your biggest need for rest?

Body   Mind   Will   Emotions

> *May God himself, the God of peace, sanctify you through and through. May your whole spirit, soul and body be kept blameless at the coming of our Lord Jesus Christ* (1 Thessalonians 5:23 NIV).

This scripture references all three parts: spirit, soul, and body. They are divinely intertwined but uniquely different in how they impact our lives.

Read Matthew 7:15-20 in your Bible.

This verse tells us that you can tell a tree (person) by its fruit. Bad trees bear bad fruit and good trees bear good fruit. The fruit of my life is produced through my belief system displayed in my words, actions and attitudes.

If we are operating out of our flesh and have an unhealthy alignment where either our soul (mind, will, and emotions) or our body is calling the shots instead of our spirit, the fruit in our lives may look like this:

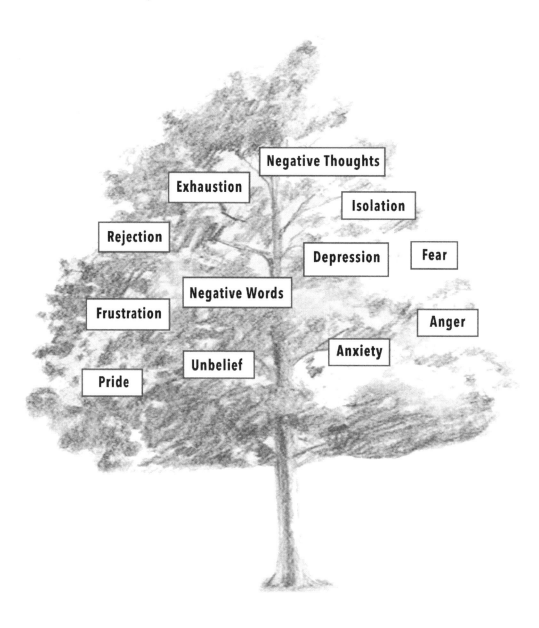

Let's look at what God reveals to us in Galatians 5 as the Fruit of the Spirit:

The Fruit of the Spirit should not be a list of pretty words hanging on a sign in our homes, but rather a description of our character that grows to become a sweet treat nourishing ourselves and others.

Our lives are producing some type of fruit. We get to regularly evaluate the fruit from our lives and take that to the Father in prayer. Being honest with ourselves, God and others about the fruit in our lives blesses everyone, especially those closest to us.

Go back to the tree and identify any of the fruit of the flesh you see in your life.

Using the chart bellow write them in:

Fruit of the Flesh in my life	Fruit of the Spirit I am asking God for
Isolation	Unity
Rejection	Acceptance
Negative Thoughts	Truth
Unbelief	Peace
	Joy

Now, read Galatians 5:22-25 circling the fruit that you are asking God to develop in you. Write those into the chart above.

> *But the Holy Spirit produces this kind of fruit in our lives: love, joy, peace, patience, kindness, goodness, faithfulness, gentleness, and self-control. There is no law against these things! Those who belong to Christ Jesus have nailed the passions and desires of their sinful nature to his cross and crucified them there. Since we are living by the Spirit, let us follow the Spirit's leading in every part of our lives (Galatians 5:22-25 NLT).*

The good news gets even better. False fruit stinks like rotten fruit because we can't keep it alive. It is God who makes things grow and gives things life. As we lean into the Father, Son and Holy Spirit, HIS FRUIT is evident. As we learn to rest in the grace, love and truth of God, the sweet aroma of fresh fruit draws others in as well.

Word of God Speak

Above all else, guard thy heart; for out of it flows the issues of life.

Proverbs 4:23 JUB

Week Three - Word of God Speak

Day One - The Word in the Beginning

The Bible is the written Word of God. There are 66 books in the Bible, 39 in the Old Testament and 27 in the New Testament. It was written over a 1500-year span by over 40 authors from different walks of life. There were kings, philosophers, shepherds, prophets and fishermen who all played a part in what we get to carry around with us as our source of truth.

The Bible is often referred to as the Word. Its existence always has been and always will be.

The Word Became Flesh

Take a look at this scripture in John:

> *In the beginning was the Word, and the Word was with God, and the Word was God. He was with God in the beginning. Through him all things were made; without him nothing was made that has been made. In him was life, and that life was the light of all mankind. The light shines in the darkness, and the darkness has not overcome it (John 1:1-6 NIV).*

The Bible tells stories and allows us to see the true nature and character of God. Jesus was the Word in human form. The prophecies about Jesus were foretold in the Old Testament (Isaiah 53), and the stories of Jesus' life, ministry, death and resurrection are told throughout the New Testament.

When you read through the four Gospels in the beginning of the New Testament, you see Matthew begins with the genealogy that led up to the life of Jesus and His birth. Mark, however, just jumped right into the climax of Jesus' life when He was baptized and started His ministry. Luke connected the dots for us as prophecies were fulfilled. And then there is John, who spends time in detail helping us understand the significance of the true identity of Jesus.

The phrase in the book of John, "in the beginning", takes us back to the very beginning of time and establishes the existence of God, the Word and the relationship between them. You cannot have one without the other. **God and the Word are eternally connected and divinely dependent on each other.**

The Word (God) became flesh (Jesus) and made His dwelling (lived) among us. The life of Jesus was foretold, but in this moment in time, God allowed men and women to experience His presence in human form. From these encounters, we have countless stories that we can build our faith on, learn from and live by.

Every word spoken about Jesus will come to fruition, and every word spoken by God through Jesus has the power to change lives.

As you read the Word, a scripture or a passage, you have the choice to read it like a book about people and events that happened long ago or read it like a love letter written by God, about God, for his children from the beginning of time until the end of time.

Did you grow up hearing or reading the Word? If so, how would you describe its place in your life?

_____

_____

_____

The Bible is God's Word for Us

As we dig into the Word, can you embrace the truth that everything inside of the book we call the Bible is from God? Is there any false belief, unbelief or question keeping you from saying yes? If so, write those down and surrender them to God. Tell Him you trust Him with those questions and ask Him to reveal Himself through them.

_____

_____

_____

_____

Every story, encounter or conversation is ordained by the God of the universe for a purpose - to impact your life. Let's walk together to discover Him as He speaks through His Word to us.

Journal about a time when God spoke directly to you through His Word.

_____
_____
_____
_____
_____
_____
_____
_____
_____
_____
_____

What is a scripture that speaks to you personally?

_____
_____
_____

Write a prayer of commitment/surrender to God to dive in head first so you can un-pack and learn to live and love the Word of God.

_____
_____
_____
_____
_____
_____
_____
_____
_____
_____
_____
_____
_____

This week's scripture we want to commit to memory is 2 Timothy 3:16. This verse reminds us of the divine purpose of the scriptures we study.

> _All scripture is God-breathed and is useful for teaching, rebuking, correcting and training in righteousness (2 Timothy 3:16 NIV)._

Week Three - Word of God Speak

The Bible is the Word of God in print form for all of us to unpack and learn from. Often times when we hear "the Word," we immediately think of a book. But the Word is so much more than a book. It is living and active, sharper than any two-edged sword.

God's Word is Living and Active

For the word of God is living and active, sharper than any two-edged sword, piercing to the division of soul and of spirit, of joints and of marrow, and discerning the thoughts and intentions of the heart (Hebrews 4:12 ESV).

Respond by journaling what this scripture means to you personally.

_____
_____

_____

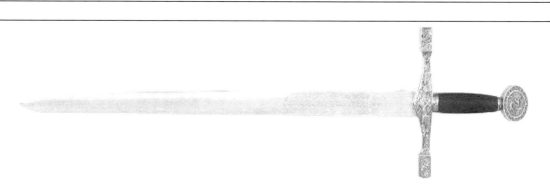

When I think of living and active, I think about a toddler who just woke up from a nap, raring and ready to go; ready to discover, encounter and embrace life. The Word of God is similar. As we read the Bible, asking Holy Spirit for revelation, there's a stirring inside of us. We get excited when we read something that brings clarity, comfort and correction to a situation or circumstance in our lives.

The Word is alive and gives life. As with any living thing, if you feed it, it grows and if you don't, it dies. We can feed our spirits with the Word of God, which is alive and active, to give life to our spirit. God's nature is firmly rooted in truth.

The word always brings truth and the truth sets us free (John 8:32 NIV).

God's Word is Absolute Truth

All Scripture is inspired by God and is useful to teach us what is true and to make us realize what is wrong in our lives. It corrects us when we are wrong and teaches us to do what is right (2 Timothy 3:16 NLT).

There is right and there is wrong in this world. There is truth that comes from one source (God Himself), and He reveals His truth to us through the Bible.

Read through this passage in Hebrews:

For the word of God is living and active, sharper than any two-edged sword, piercing to the division of soul and of spirit, of joints and of marrow, and discerning the thoughts and intentions of the heart. And no creature is hidden from his sight, but all are naked and exposed to the eyes of him to whom we must give account. Since then we have a great high priest who has passed through the heavens, Jesus, the Son of God, let us hold fast our confession. For we do not have a high priest who is unable to sympathize with our weaknesses, but one who in every respect has been tempted as we are, yet without sin. Let us then with confidence draw near to the throne of grace, that we may receive mercy and find grace to help in time of need (Hebrews 4:1-16 ESV).

The Word is alive in us. Anything that we have is planted by reading, praying, discussing and unpacking the Word and is used by God in our everyday lives. This scripture points out the ability of the Word in us. Through the words we read in the Bible, hear preached on Sundays or spoken in daily conversation, Holy Spirit can prompt our spirit and will gently move us to line up with His truth. The Word of God is truth, and when overlaid in any situation will show us the lies of the world and the enemy we have partnered with.

Because we are made up of three parts, body, soul and spirit, this scripture is referring to dividing soul and spirit. Our soul is our mind, will and emotions. Our spirit as believers is directly connected to His Spirit. We live in a human body made of flesh in a broken world. The Word divides soul and spirit and discerns the motive of the heart.

In what ways are you allowing yourself to be soul-led (living by your mind/will/emotions) instead of being spirit-led?

_____

_____

_____

_____

_____

_____

Do you regularly evaluate the intentions of your heart with the truth of the Word and the gracious love of God?

_____

_____

Are there any self-condemning thoughts that you are believing that don't line up with the Word of God?

_____

_____

_____

_____

_____

_____

Spend a few minutes just talking about this with God through prayer. Tell Him about any weaknesses in you and let Him cover them with His love and truth.

Take a minute and look at this week's verse. Hopefully you're working on hiding this scripture in your heart.

All scripture is God - breathed and is useful for teaching, rebuking, and correcting and training in righteousness.

2 Timothy 3:16 NIV

Week Three - Word of God Speak

Day Three - Hide God's Word in our Hearts

The Word of God is a gift given to us from the heart of our loving Father. When we value something, we make it a priority. In the same way, something that is a priority to us gets our time and attention. As we learn to make reading, studying and knowing the Word of God a priority, it will be in our head, heart and spill over into our lives.

> *Jesus answered, "It is written: Man shall not live on bread alone, but on every word that comes from the mouth of God" (Matthew 4:4 NIV).*

Fix God's Word on our Hearts

Take a few minutes and read through Deuteronomy 6:6-9 (NIV).

> *Fix these words of mine in your hearts and minds; tie them as symbols on your hands and bind them on your foreheads. Teach them to your children, talking about them when you sit at home and when you walk along the road, when you lie down and when you get up. Write them on the doorframes of your houses and on your gates, so that your days and the days of your children may be many in the land the LORD swore to give your ancestors, as many as the days that the heavens are above the earth.*

Deuteronomy 6 is a favorite passage for parents or ministers who work with families. Many sermons are preached through this passage from the angle of the role of the parent. If you have kids and a desire to raise them to know and love Jesus, these helpful tips from the Bible become your play-book. But like any well planned play-book, the plays are only as powerful as the skills of the players.

The Word of God can be described as a map to give us directions on where to go, a mirror to use to examine our hearts and motives, and a play-book that teaches us how to win at life.

Verse 6 is often overlooked as you get into the "how to." The instruction is clear. Before we can teach them to our spiritual or physical children, we must first fix them in our hearts.

> *Above all else, guard thy heart; for out of it flows the issues of life* (Proverbs 4:23 JUB).

In Deuteronomy, God is telling us to put His words in our hearts, teach them to our children and talk about them as we go through life because as we see in Proverbs 4:23, that "*…out of it flows the issues of life*", and also in Luke 6:45, *A good man produces good out of the good storeroom of his heart… for his mouth speaks from the overflow of the heart.* What is in our hearts comes out.

Let's ponder this: many of us decorate our homes with our favorite scriptures and sayings, but have we decorated the walls of our home with more scripture than the walls of our hearts? God desires for us to read the Bible, study and memorize it, so that we can know His nature and character. As we do this, the Word becomes a part of us. We fix these words in our hearts and minds, so that we can have an intimate relationship with God, ourselves and others.

To practice fixing God's Word on our hearts and minds, we must meditate on it, keep it in front of us all the time, and speak it to all who are around us. Every week we introduce the weekly scripture, so you will have a verse to commit to memory. By the end of this book, you will have at least eight scriptures that you have hidden in your heart that will come to mind when you need them. You may have noticed that we have emphasized memorizing this week's scripture three days in a row because we want to equip you to truly embrace the practice of *hiding God's word in our hearts.*

This week's scripture is 2 Timothy 3:16 (NIV).

> *All scripture is God - breathed and is useful for teaching, rebuking, correcting and training in righteousness.*

Remember, God hasn't called us to only read the Bible, but to also study it so that we can know His nature and character! As we do this, the Word becomes a part of us. We will fix His words on our hearts and minds.

A few helpful tips for memorizing scripture:

- Write it on a note-card and put it on your mirror so you read it every time you look at yourself.

- Write it on a Post-it Note®, stick it to the dash in your car and read it out loud a few times every day.

- Take a photo of the scripture or find an image with the scripture and save it as your lock screen on your phone, so every time you look at your phone you will see it.

Today we want you to practice doing exactly what the scripture tells you to do. Write this week's memory verse 2 Timothy 3:16 in the heart below.

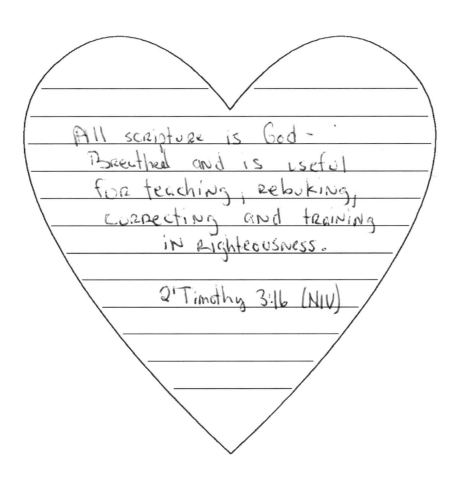

All scripture is God-Breathed and is useful for teaching, rebuking, correcting and training in Righteousness.

2'Timothy 3:16 (NIV)

Week Three - Word of God Speak

Day Four - The Old and New Testament

The Old Testament and the New Testament are distinctly different but perfectly complement each other. There are approximately 250 Old Testament scriptures quoted in the New Testament and more than 1000 New Testament references to things written in the Old Testament.

The Old Testament Law

In week one, we talked about sin entering the world. This was the moment everything shifted, and we collided head on with the hardships of life. Unity with our Creator was disrupted by sin.

"You will not certainly die," the serpent said to the woman in Genesis 3:4.

This was the genesis moment Eve believed the lie of the enemy and ate of the fruit sharing it with her husband. The disunity between God and man began. The Old Testament recounts the events that followed including the giving of God's law and man's inability to live up to it. The Old Testament reveals God's wrath towards sin as a rebellious nation fails to keep His commands. Prophets continue to proclaim the coming of the Messiah as the Israelite people wait, and God in His unending mercy continues to protect and provide for His people.

> Jesus said *"Do not think that I have come to abolish the Law or the prophets; I have not come to abolish them, but to fulfill them"* (Matthew 5:17 NIV).

The stories and prophecies in the Old Testament point to the coming Christ and the new covenant where faith alone will save us. The sacrifice of the Messiah in the New Testament restores unity with God and creates in us a temple for the Holy Spirit to dwell. With the fulfillment of the Law, Jesus also makes a way that ALL may know God including Gentiles. **God's grace is poured out on mankind through Jesus.**

What is your favorite Old Testament story? What do you think that story was trying to teach us about the coming of Jesus?

_____

_____

The New Testament Promise

Let's look at a couple of ways Jesus fulfilled, in the New Testament, the law and prophecies found in the Old Testament.

The Law
Moses ascends the mountain to retrieve the law which regulates Old Testament life. The Old Testament reveals man's inability to follow the law.

> *Therefore no one will be declared righteous in God's sight by the works of the law; rather, through the law we become conscious of our sin* (Romans 3:20 NIV).

The New Testament reveals that the law was never meant to save but to reveal a savior. Faith in Him alone will bring our salvation.

> *That if you confess with your mouth, "Jesus is Lord," and believe in your heart that God raised him from the dead, you will be saved. For it is with your heart that you believe and are justified, and it is with your mouth that you confess and are saved* (Romans 10:9-10 NIV).

The Shedding of Blood
Many times, in the Old Testament, the sacrifice of blood is illustrated. It is very clear that without the shedding of blood, there can be no forgiveness of sin. The last plague of Egypt that would set the Israelites free was the Plague of the firstborn where every firstborn son was killed. Every Israelite family was to take a lamb without defect and raise it until the day of Passover when they would slaughter the lamb and place the blood over their door, and death would not touch their home. This is a foreshadowing of the sacrifice of Jesus.

> *Our sins are washed away and we are made clean because Christ gave His own body as a gift to God. He did this once for all time* (Hebrews 10:10 NLT).

The blood shed by Jesus took on all sin for all time. He took on all of God's wrath towards sin and poured out all of God's grace upon believers.

Relationship with God restored

> *God made him who had no sin to be sin for us, so that in him we might become the righteousness of God* (2 Corinthians 5:21 NIV).

God's plan has always been redemption. He wanted to restore us to Him. He gave us Jesus, so we could know Him personally and intimately.

The separation brought about by sin meant that man could no longer walk with God as in the garden. His glory would literally cause people to fall over dead. In Exodus 40, God instructs Moses on how to create the Tabernacle with the Holy of Holies being in the innermost place where only the high priest could enter. This pattern of worship would continue until Jesus died, and the veil separating us from God was torn (Matthew 27:51). We no longer need to approach God through a high priest. Jesus became our high priest, this allows us to *approach God's throne of grace with confidence, so that we may receive mercy and find grace to help us in our time of need* (Hebrews 4:16).

Read Hebrews 4:14-16. Do you approach God with confidence? Do you still see God as someone who is finding fault with you or waiting to receive you with love? Journal your thoughts below:

_____
_____
_____
_____
_____
_____

The Old Testament chronicles countless stories of God's provision, protection and healing while the New Testament shows how Jesus becomes our provision, protection, healer, and redeemer. He made a way, so we could come boldly before the throne of grace.

Take a minute and write out some of the ways you've experienced God's provision, protection, healing, redemption, and grace in your life.

_____
_____
_____
_____
_____
_____

Week Three - Word of God Speak

Day Five - How to Study the Word

We can't tell you *what* to do without telling you *how* to do it. Today we are going to spend some time talking practically about how to dive into and study the Word of God.

> *All Scripture is God-breathed and is useful for teaching, rebuking, correcting and training in righteousness, so that the servant of God may be thoroughly equipped for every good work (2 Timothy 3:16-17 NIV).*

According to the verse above, what are the four things the scripture is useful for?
_____, _____, _____ & _____

The Bible can be an overwhelming book. Isaiah alone has 66 chapters. The good news is that the Word of God is given to us as a gift, breathed out by our Creator for our good, so that we may know Him more. Choosing to follow Jesus does not require you to be a Bible scholar, but you will find that as your heart is transformed, the desire to know the God-breathed Word begins to burn inside of you. So where do you begin?

Carve out time to study

Even with a desire to know God more, the distractions of life can hijack our time and focus. When we have made the decision to know God more through His Word, we get to reorient our schedules to make room. For some, that means getting up earlier than everyone else in your house. For others, it is mid-morning when chores are done, and the house is quiet. Perhaps it is first thing when you arrive at the office, before you dive into your duties for the day. It can also be in your car on the way to work or in the evening before you go to bed. Maybe you have a lunch hour where you can quietly read in your office. Whatever the time, it is important to commit to it, or we can lose the passion we once had as it's drowned out by the world around us.

When and where do you carve out time to study?_____

If you haven't already, let's make a commitment together. Where and when can you carve out time to get in the Word?_____

**BONUS: Now take it a step further and put that as a recurring event on your calendar or write it in your planner as a reminder.

Start with your Bible

Do you have a Bible that you are comfortable reading and studying? Almost every Bible has footnotes with cross references that can start you on a journey of discovery. As you dig in, He will bring revelation and truth. We suggest a study Bible that will include tools such as concordances, indexes, glossaries and other helpful references for understanding the Word. Pick a translation that makes sense to you. When you are picking a Bible, it is always helpful to read a familiar passage and the scriptures around it to make sure it's a good fit for you.

Just start reading. Wherever you start is a good start, but sometimes we need a little direction. The New Testament can help you in your understanding of His great LOVE for us. The gospel of John is a great place to begin! You can read the story of Jesus' life. All four gospels, Matthew, Mark, Luke and John, retell the story of Jesus' birth, ministry and ultimately his death for our sins from different perspectives. Through the gospels you will find reference to the Old Testament. For example, Jesus refers to Old Testament verses that would have been written in the Torah (the first five books of the Old Testament) when He is tempted by satan (Matthew 4). As you read these verses, use the references to go find the Old Testament verses. Finding this connection between the Old and New Covenant (law and grace) encourages more discovery. Without any resource other than the Bible itself, you have started to study the Word!

Other Resources

After becoming more comfortable with the Word itself, you may want to dive into concordances, Biblical dictionaries, devotionals or commentaries. There are many books available and many resources are available online such as Blue Letter Bible App (blueletterbible.org) or biblestudytools.com. These resources can often help explain some of the cultural or time-specific things that are happening in the Bible.

God's Word allows us to understand His character and discern the truth. It is a weapon against the schemes of the enemy (Hebrews 4:12). Ask God to create the desire inside of you to know more of Him. Ask Him to show you where He wants you to begin and allow the Word of God to draw you deeper into a relationship with Him.

Make a plan and write it down. Share it with a friend you trust for accountability and encouragement.

I am going to share my plan with _____

Remember this: Jesus doesn't want to be a check on your to-do list. He wants to be in a relationship with you!

God speaks when we study His word

Week Three - Word of God Speak

Day Six - Resting My Mind

Because our soul is made up of three parts, mind, will and emotions, we must take time to engage and disengage all three. Our emotions show up the loudest when we are in a place of unrest, and the enemy loves to wreak havoc in our minds.

What does a mind at rest look and feel like?

_____

For me, when my mind is going in so many directions at a speed I feel like I can't keep up with, my emotions kick in. Serving on the ministry team at elevateHim, we are called to promote, encourage and connect. It is a privilege to get to do what we do, but there's so much more involved than many realize. It's easy to let our minds race with responsibilities, new ideas, heavy burdens and brainstorming. It's ALL a part of what we get to do, but we can't do it all at once. We are learning as a team what it means to rest in the few things God has asked us to say yes to RIGHT NOW. As we do this, we have more clarity and focus for the things right in front of us instead of fragmented thoughts that lead to frustration.

At elevateHim we have a weekly staff meeting where we come together to plan and pray. There have been times when we've had to stop a meeting to refocus and ask Holy Spirit what we are supposed to do next. There have been other times when we have committed to fast in unity as a team or take a day to GO TO THE WOODS about a specific topic, direction or decision. All of these practices allow us to rest our minds. What are we resting in? HIM. We are resting in Him to quiet our minds and speak directly to our hearts. What are we resting on? We are resting on the truth and promises from the Word to sustain us, give us wisdom and provide a stable foundation for us to build our lives on. Who comforts us in our rest? The Holy Spirit meets us in the place of rest and ministers to us.

Write down all the thoughts racing through your mind right now when it comes to your life, your family, your job, your responsibilities, your dreams and your concerns.

- _____

- _____

- _____

- _____

- _____

- _____

Proverbs 3:5-6 (NIV) tells us to *"Trust in the Lord with all your heart and lean not on your own understanding. In all your ways acknowledge Him and He will make your path straight."*

Now, one by one, out loud, tell the Lord you trust Him with each one of the things on your list.

"Lord, I trust you with _____ "

"Lord, I trust you with _____ "

"Lord, I trust you with _____ "

"Lord, I trust you with _____ "

"Lord, I trust you with _____ "

"Lord, I trust you with _____ "

After you release them, take a deep breath and rest your mind. You no longer have to think about, over-analyze, or stress over these things because God is big enough. As you rest in Him, He will give you the wisdom, strength and courage to tackle each one of them!

Grace, Love and Holy Spirit

Hearing God

A personal timely word from God changes circumstances.

Grace, Love and Holy Spirit

Week Four - Hearing God

Day One - Hearing God through Prayer

HEARING GOD IS A TWO-WAY CONVERSATION THAT MUST BE ENGAGED THROUGH PRAYER.

Hearing God looks different for each of us, but is one of the most important investments we can make.

- Hearing God can be sitting quietly in the stillness.
- Hearing God can be driving down the road talking to Him.
- Hearing God can be conversation with Him throughout your day.
- Hearing God can be fasting to create more space to hear Him.
- Hearing God can be digging into the Word for clarity.
- Hearing God can be stopping mid-yell when you're losing it on your kids and walking into the other room.
- Hearing God can be choosing to turn around and walk in the opposite direction of your biggest temptation.

Hearing God looks different for everyone, but the one thing that remains the same…He speaks, we listen…we speak, He listens. He speaks, we respond.

Life is a constant two-way conversation with God. It works just like every other healthy relationship in our lives.

So why is prayer such a big deal? Why does it matter if I talk to God on a daily basis?

In the Old Testament, before Jesus came to earth in human form, God's people could not address Him in conversation or worship directly. There was always a go-between, a priest who sacrificed on their behalf, in order to make people righteous in God's eyes. Enter onto the scene, Jesus, the perfect and ultimate sacrifice.

He took the place of every animal sacrifice ever required to commune with God personally, taking out the middleman. Because His sacrifice of dying on a cross was absolutely perfect, He settled the debt that sin held against us, removing the very thing that kept us from our God.

Jesus was the key that unlocked prayer becoming our final priest needed to bridge the gap between God and us.

Our connection with God came at such a high price, that in itself illustrates the value in which God saw prayer. We get to view it as a privilege and grace that we are afforded the opportunity to commune and converse with God directly. We get to take our own needs and the needs of others to the throne of grace.

A few things you need to know about prayer:

Prayer is Giving Thanks

> *Do not be anxious about anything, but in every situation, by prayer and petition, with thanksgiving, present your requests to God. And the peace of God, which transcends all understanding, will guard your hearts and your minds in Christ Jesus (Philippians 4:6-7 NIV).*

Our greatest response to the love of God is to offer up a prayer of praise. Praise, by definition, is the act of expressing admiration, approval and to glorify. We can offer praise to our Creator through prayer. Every day we have a standing invitation to converse with Him, thank Him for who He is, how we've seen Him at work in our lives and acknowledge His love.

Prayer is Relational

> *If you remain in me and my words remain in you, ask whatever you wish, and it will be done for you (John 15:7 NIV).*

> *Let us then approach God's throne of grace with confidence, so that we may receive mercy and find grace to help us in our time of need (Hebrews 4:16 NIV).*

> *Ask and it will be given to you; seek and you will find; knock and the door will be opened to you. For everyone who asks receives; the one who seeks finds; and to the one who knocks, the door will be opened (Matthew 7:7 NIV).*

God is not interested in our recitation of words or in thoughtless prayers that do not connect with our hearts. There is nothing fancy or strict about the way we interact with God. The way we talk with a friend using language we would normally use in conversation is the easiest entry point. We approach God in prayer by talking about our day, our worries, our triumphs and struggles without fear of judgment or repercussion. We get to bring all of our concerns to Him and ask Him for guidance, healing or even correction.

What do you need to ask God for today? List out the most obvious struggles in your life currently and ask God to begin working on your behalf. Next, list out different struggles or need that may not be as obvious such as a past sin, a spiritual hurt, even an addiction. Be bold enough to pray for that as well.

- _____
- _____
- _____

- _____
- _____
- _____

Prayer Brings Protection

Finally, be strong in the Lord and in his mighty power. Put on the full armor of God, so that you can take your stand against the devil's schemes. For our struggle is not against flesh and blood, but against the rulers, against the authorities, against the powers of this dark world and against the spiritual forces of evil in the heavenly realms (Ephesians 6:10-12 NIV).

To battle in a spiritual war, we must put on armor in a spiritual manner. In this case, prayer is how we suit up for the fight. We also pray for the protection of others. It is our privilege and responsibility to pray for our families, our churches, our leaders in government and believers across the world. The protection afforded by prayer is immeasurable!

Look up the different parts of the armor of God listed in Ephesians 6:14-17. Picture in your mind putting on all the pieces of armor while praying aloud for God to use those pieces to protect you. As a believer I have access to put on the full armor of God and keep it on. Each piece will protect me and equip me for every battle I will face.

Prayer is Powerful

> *Therefore, confess your sins to each other and pray for each other so that you may be healed. The prayer of a righteous person is powerful and effective* (James 5:16 NIV).

Many times, what is emphasized in this scripture is the word "confess." In many cases, it becomes a to-do list, or worse, a law that must be accomplished first before we can hear God. God has already forgiven you as a follower of Christ for your past, present and future sins. The word we want to highlight is **"prayer."** After many years of ministering, I now see this scripture as a call to partner with God's grace in relationship with yourself and others. We have been given the righteousness of Christ. When we pray over someone who is in need, we have the power of Jesus and His righteousness in our words. Confession then becomes more about transparency and vulnerability rather than a law, and prayer becomes more about His righteousness and His power.

We have been given a gift and an opportunity to pray for each other for a wide array of needs: healing, clarity, growth, passion, believing that God will give us what we ask for in prayer.

When was the last time you felt powerful in prayer? What holds you back from seeing results from your prayers? Journal your response below.

_____

_____

_____

End today with writing out your prayers. Tell Him what you're thankful for, why you love Him and what you need. Surrender your burdens and thank Him for His faithfulness that will move mountains in your life and in the lives of those you're praying for.

_____

_____

_____

This week we will memorize Jeremiah 33:3. This verse is a great reminder that He will speak to us so that we can hear Him when we do our part…to call to Him.

> *Call to me and I will answer you, and will tell you great and hidden things that you have not known (Jeremiah 33:3 ESV).*

Week Four - Hearing God

Day Two - God Speaks, We Listen

The subject of prayer should be simple, but many people have complicated the issue with lofty and eloquent speech such as was reserved for our founding fathers or seventeenth century poets, as well as rules of how to and not to approach God in prayer. In week seven, we will cover our identity in Christ in great detail, but remember when it comes to prayer; we are children of God. We are talking to our Father.

One of the best examples of this is seen in The Message version of Romans.

> *This resurrection life you received from God is not a timid, grave-tending life. It's adventurously expectant, greeting God with a childlike "What's next, Papa?" God's Spirit touches our spirits and confirms who we really are. We know who He is, and we know who we are: Father and children* (Romans 8:15-17a MSG).

When we understand this, then we can tackle the question of how He speaks to us, His children. First things first, if you or someone you know has never heard God speak, then we are compelled to ask a fundamental question, "Are you His child?"

> *My sheep hear My voice, I know them, and they follow Me* (John 10:27 HCSB).

Jesus' sheep are the children of God, people who have answered His salvation call and hear His voice! But even if you have not done that, it is not as bad as you think.

> *If you declare with your mouth, "Jesus is Lord," and believe in your heart that God raised Him from the dead, you will be saved. For it is with your heart that you believe and are justified, and it is with your mouth that you profess your faith and are saved* (Romans 10:9-10 NIV).

Salvation is as simple as that, and once received, you are one of His sheep.

> *God is not a man who lies, or a son of man who changes His mind. Does He speak and not act, or promise and not fulfill?* (Numbers 23:19 HCSB).

If God says His sheep hear His voice, then they do, can, and will.

At the beginning of this study, we reviewed how God in Genesis chapter one would say, *"Let there be…"* and whatever He said was. In John 1:1-3, it says, *"In the beginning was the Word, and the Word was with God, and the Word was God. He was in the beginning with God. All things were made through Him, and without Him nothing was made that was made (NKJV)."* Then in John 1:14 it says, *"And the Word became flesh and dwelt among us, and we beheld His glory, the glory as of the only begotten of the Father, full of grace and truth (NKJV)."*

God the Father created with words. Jesus was with the Father from the beginning and is the *Logos* Word (living embodiment of the constant written word), and in John 14:26 Jesus says *"…the Holy Spirit, whom the Father will send in my name, will teach you all things and will remind you of everything I have said to you…"* (NIV).

The above scriptures reinforce the premise that God is always speaking and communicating with us. We just need to open our spiritual ears and eyes to see and hear Him.

Just as earthly parents communicate to children in many ways, so does our Heavenly Father. As with anyone you desire to communicate, the first step is to make sure you recognize their language. We often forget that God doesn't speak as we do, and His first language isn't always English, but He is always speaking.

In Job 38:1 (MSG), we see that God answered Job from the eye of a violent storm…

Romans 1:20a (NIV) tells us that God is clearly seen in creation. John 14:25-26 tells us that God's Holy Spirit lives inside of us, communicates with our spirit, teaches us, guides us, and comforts us. In 1 Kings 19:12 God speaks in a still small voice. Dreams and visions are another way that God can communicate to us.

> *"And it shall come to pass in the last days,"* says God, *"That I will pour out of My Spirit on all flesh; Your sons and your daughters shall prophesy, your young men shall see visions, your old men shall dream*

dreams. And on My menservants and on My maidservants, I will pour out My Spirit in those days; And they shall prophesy. I will show wonders in heaven above and signs in the earth beneath: Blood and fire and vapor of smoke. The sun shall be turned into darkness, And the moon into blood, Before the coming of the great and awesome day of the Lord. And it shall come to pass That whoever calls on the name of the Lord Shall be saved" (Acts 2:17-21 NKJV).

The important thing to remember is that He is always speaking and communicating to us. We just don't always recognize it. Once we are saved, we have assurance that we are His sheep. Because this is our truth, how can we tune our spiritual ears to hear Him better?

We get a clue in Romans 10:17. We are going to look at several versions of this scripture to get a complete understanding of what is being said.

> **Romans 10:17:**
> *So then faith cometh by hearing, and hearing by the word of God* (KJV).
>
> *So faith comes from hearing, and hearing through the word of Christ* (ESV).
>
> *Therefore faith is from the hearing ear, and the hearing ear is from the word of God* (ABPE).

I am going to simplify this verse even more. **Faith increases when we hear God. We grow our faith by hearing God**. If you want to hear God, get familiar with His Word. His Word is His voice speaking to us. Everything He tells you will line up with His Word.

We are going to spend the rest of this week focusing on how God speaks through His written Word (*logos*), by His Spirit through revelation/spoken word (*rhēma*), and through His people as prophecy.

When we just read the Word, we can miss the heart of God by rushing through it. We get to study, reflect on, meditate on and marinate in the Word to give us wisdom, insight and instruction.

Remember prayer is talking to God and listening to His voice for wisdom and instruction. Hearing God is a crucial part of our relationship with Him. Do you feel like you hear God? Write a prayer below asking Him to speak to you in fresh and new ways this week. Share your thoughts, gratitude, and even frustrations with Him in regards to prayer and hearing Him.

_____
_____
_____
_____
_____
_____
_____
_____
_____
_____
_____
_____
_____
_____
_____
_____
_____
_____
_____
_____
_____
_____
_____
_____
_____
_____
_____
_____
_____
_____
_____
_____
_____
_____
_____

Week Four - Hearing God

Day Three - Hearing God Through His Word

Yesterday we reviewed a few scriptures about how to increase our ability to hear God. Romans 10:17 tells us that faith is increased from hearing God, and the ability to hear God comes from familiarity with His Word.

The Written Word

The written Word (or *logos* - Bible) is often our first introduction to God's language. It's no ordinary book as we see in Hebrews 4:12 because it is alive and active.

> *For the word of God is living and active, sharper than any two-edged sword, piercing to the division of soul and of spirit, of joints and of marrow, and discerning the thoughts and intentions of the heart* (Hebrews 4:12 ESV).

It's inspiring to see Jesus living out the instructions God has given us from the beginning of time. It is mind blowing to me that the one who is the Word in the flesh took the time to sit and listen to the Word of God. Let's look at a story about Jesus as a boy from Luke.

> *When He was 12 years old, they went up according to the custom of the festival. After those days were over, as they were returning, the boy Jesus stayed behind in Jerusalem, but His parents did not know it. Assuming He was in the traveling party, they went a day's journey. Then they began looking for Him among their relatives and friends. When they did not find Him, they returned to Jerusalem to search for Him. After three days,* **they found Him in the temple complex sitting among the teachers, listening to them and asking them questions.** *And all those who heard Him were astounded at His understanding and His answers. When His parents saw Him, they were*

astonished, and His mother said to Him, "Son, why have You treated us like this? Your father and I have been anxiously searching for You." "Why were you searching for Me?" He asked them. "Didn't you know that I had to be in My Father's house?" But they did not understand what He said to them. Then He went down with them and came to Nazareth and was obedient to them. His mother kept all these things in her heart. **And Jesus increased in wisdom and stature, and in favor with God and with people** (Luke 2:42-52 HCS).

We see that Jesus grew in wisdom, age, and favor with both God and people. The word for favor is also translated as grace. We can grow in wisdom and favor as well by reading, studying and applying the Word of God.

Do you ever wonder why some concepts come so naturally to certain people, and others get a revelation later? A few of our kids grasped this concept early. They had such an innate comprehension of the importance of the Word of God that whenever they were frightened at night, they would sleep with a Bible under their pillow. It was as if they believed it would sink in by osmosis, and just the physical presence of the Word under their pillow would be enough to protect them. But such is childlike faith…childlike faith will cling to something because it knows there is power without the need of understanding.

In Matthew 4, when Jesus is tempted by satan in the wilderness, He combats temptation by answering satan with the Word.

> *"It is written… Man shall not live on bread alone but on every word that comes from the mouth of God"* (Matthew 4:4 NIV).

> *"It is also written: Do not put the Lord your Go to the test"* (Matthew 4:7 NIV).

> *"…for it is written: Worship the Lord your God and serve only him"* (Matthew 4:10 NIV).

Jesus also said, *"…I did not speak on my own, but the Father who sent me commanded me to say all that I have spoken"* (John 12:49 NIV). Therefore, we can surmise that the Father told Jesus to combat satan with Scripture.

We Know God through His Word

The way God speaks through His Word can take many forms. Through study and familiarity, we get a better picture of the nature and character of God. *In the beginning was the Word, and the Word was with God, and the Word was God* (John 1:1 KJV). Remember that this verse is talking about Jesus.

One of the ways God speaks to me through the Word is with what I like to call "highlighter moments." I will read a passage or scripture that I have read before, but it will be as if the Holy Spirit highlighted a portion of it. I will usually see that scripture from a fresh perspective or in a way I had not noticed it before. Sometimes I gather new meaning; sometimes it prepares me for something that is in my future.

A fairly recent example of this happened about 10 months ago. I was busy trying to study and prepare according to my own plan, and I heard God say to me, "*My grace is sufficient for you… in every situation and every season.*" I remember responding, "I know Lord, You're always good." In the spirit of transparency and honesty, I ignored it, until I heard God repeat this same sentence to me three more times. Then I stopped what I was doing and opened my Bible.

The first part of His statement is a familiar verse, I know this verse:

> *But he said to me, "My grace is sufficient for you, for power is perfected in weakness." Therefore, I will most gladly boast all the more about my weakness, so that Christ's power may reside in me. So, because of Christ, I am pleased in weakness, in insults, in catastrophes, in persecutions, and in pressures. For when I am weak, then I am strong* (2 Corinthians 12:9-10 HCSB).

God went on to teach me through study and break-down of verse 9, that His grace, which is loving-kindness and favor and what He uses to draw people to Himself, will keep me, strengthen me, increase my faith, knowledge and affection, and it cannot fail me. **His powerful strength is the nature of who He is.** His grace also contains strength, which is the power to perform miracles, and command the strength of armies. His strength is perfect in my weakness (or surrendering situations to Him).

God knows my future and what is coming next. Twenty-four hours after this encounter with God, my Mom was diagnosed with cancer and about 48 hours after that we found that it had spread throughout most of her body. God knew exactly what I needed to hear, and He used His Word to communicate love and comfort to me in preparation for what was ahead. Without a familiarity, I am not sure I would have heard Him so clearly. It was this familiarity that allowed me to recognize what He was saying because it sounded like Him. Because His voice is familiar I could hear what He was saying to me.

Is there a situation in your life where you need to apply the Word? Journal below.

_____

_____

_____

_____

_____

_____

Let's read a few scriptures about the Word of God:

> *All Scripture is God-breathed and is useful for teaching, rebuking, correcting and training in righteousness, so that the servant of God may be thoroughly equipped for every good work (2 Timothy 3:16-17 NIV).*

> *I have hidden your word in my heart that I might not sin against you (Psalm 119:11 NIV).*

> *Your word is a lamp for my feet, a light on my path (Psalms 119:105 NIV).*

> *The unfolding of your words gives light; it gives understanding to the simple (Psalms 119:130 NIV).*

> *In the beginning was the Word, and the Word was with God, and the Word was God (John 1:1 NIV).*

> *The Word became flesh and made his dwelling among us. We have seen his glory, the glory of the one and only Son, who came from the Father, full of grace and truth (John 1:14 NIV).*

> *If you remain in me and my words remain in you, ask whatever you wish, and it will be done for you (John 15:7 NIV).*

> *All your words are true; all your righteous laws are eternal (Psalm 119:160 NIV).*

> *Every word of God is flawless; he is a shield to those who take refuge in him (Proverbs 30:5 NIV).*

As you go through your day meditate on this:

> *The instruction of the Lord is perfect, renewing one's life; the testimony of the Lord is trustworthy, making the inexperienced wise. The precepts of the Lord are right, making the heart glad; the command of the Lord is radiant, making the eyes light up. The fear of the Lord is pure, enduring forever; the ordinances of the Lord are reliable and altogether righteous. They are more desirable than gold— than an abundance of pure gold; and sweeter than honey, which comes from the honeycomb. In addition, your servant is warned by them; there is great reward in keeping them (Psalms 19:7-11 HCSB).*

According to the above scriptures, we learn that His Word can be so many things to us. Circle what you need His Word to be for you.

What is your favorite scripture and why?

_____
_____
_____
_____

Can you remember a time God spoke directly to your heart through His Word? Journal about that below.

_____
_____
_____
_____
_____
_____
_____

Take a moment and journal below about an area of your life you want to grow in hearing Him through His Word.

_____
_____
_____
_____
_____
_____
_____

Week Four - Hearing God

Day Four - Hearing God Through His Spirit

"God still speaks to men and women every day! The question shouldn't be if God still speaks. 'Are we listening?' is the real question!" elevateHim

When talking about the Word of God or getting a word from God, there are typically two Greek words, *logos* and *rhēma*, that are both translated as word but have different meanings. To adequately explain this concept, we need to look at the original definition of these words.

Understanding *Logos* and *Rhēma*

These words are often used synonymously in the New Testament. The word *logos* is a masculine noun (Strong's G3056), used 330 times, and generally refers to the complete or constant written or spoken Word of God. Most people understand it to be the written Word of God, but in actuality, it is much more than that. This word is used to describe Jesus in John 1, who is the living Word. Let's take a look at a few examples of the use of *logos*:

> *In the beginning was the Word [logos], and the Word [logos] was with God, and the Word [logos] was God* (John 1:1 NKJV).

> *For the word [logos] of God is living and effective and sharper than any double-edged sword, penetrating as far as the separation of soul and spirit, joints and marrow. It is able to judge the ideas and thoughts of the heart* (Hebrews 4:12 HCSB).

> *Being born again, not of corruptible seed, but of incorruptible, by the word [logos] of God, which liveth and abideth forever* (1 Peter 1:23 NKJV).

Rhēma is a Greek neutral noun (Strong's G4487), used 70 times in the New Testament and is indicative of a spoken or uttered word. Another way to say this is *rhēma* is God speaking to us personally. Examples of *rhēma* in scripture are:

> *So then faith comes by hearing, and hearing by the word [rhēma] of God* (Romans 10:17 NKJV).

> *If you abide in Me, and My words [rhēma] abide in you, you will ask what you desire, and it shall be done for you* (John 15:7 NKJV).

> *Husbands love your wives, just as Christ also loved the church and gave Himself for her, that He might sanctify and cleanse her with the washing of water by the word [rhēma]* (Ephesians 5:25-26 NIV).

> *And Peter remembered the word [rhēma], of Jesus who had said to him, "Before the rooster crows, you will deny Me three times." So he went out and wept bitterly* (Matthew 26:75 NKJV).

> *Mary said, Behold the handmaid of the Lord; be it unto me according to thy word [rhēma]* (Luke 1:38 NKJV).

Peter Encounters the Word

Do you remember the story about the first time Jesus and Peter met?

> *As the crowd was pressing in on Jesus to hear God's word [logos], He was standing by Lake Gennesaret. He saw two boats at the edge of the lake; the fishermen had left them and were washing their nets. He got into one of the boats, which belonged to Simon, and asked him to put out a little from the land. Then He sat down and was teaching the crowds from the boat. When He had finished speaking, He said to Simon, "Put out into deep water and let down your nets for a catch." "Master," Simon replied, "we've worked hard all night long and caught nothing! But at Your word [rhēma], I'll let down the nets." When they did this, they caught a great number of fish, and their nets began to tear. So they signaled to their partners in the other boat to come and help them; they came and filled both boats so full that they began to sink. When Simon Peter saw this, he fell at Jesus' knees and said, "Go away from me, because I'm a sinful man, Lord!" For he and all those with him were amazed at the catch of fish they took, and so were James and John, Zebedee's sons, who were Simon's partners* (Luke 5:1-11 HCSB).

Let me give you a recap of the events: the Word, Jesus, had been speaking to the crowd and teaching them precepts from the written word. When He was finished, He (Jesus) turns to Simon Peter and gives him a *rhēma* word, a word spoken to him and his situation. That word was, "Put out into deep water and let down your nets for a catch." Peter acted in faith and said, *"…at Your word [rhēma], I'll let down the nets."* Peter's situation changed in an instant. **A personal timely Word from God changes circumstances** and, as seen in Romans 10:17 (NKJV), *So then faith comes by hearing, and hearing by the word [rhēma] of God,* builds faith. Hearing the *rhēma* word built Peter's faith, and because he was acting in faith, Peter caught so many fish his nets began to tear. A key thing to see in this story is that Jesus was teaching *logos*, before He gave *rhēma*.

Holy Spirit is the person of the Godhead that dwells in us and is with us wherever we go. Because these three are one (the Father, Jesus, & the Holy Spirit), we often use these terms synonymously. Often Holy Spirit uses *logos* (written word) to speak *rhēma* (a personal word) to us.

Scripture may stand out in a way it never has before and apply to your current situation. You may hear a scripture spoken in your mind. A *rhēma* word is never contradictory to *logos*. We see this in scripture in 1 John 5:7 which says, *For there are three that bear witness in heaven: the Father, the Word, and the Holy Spirit; and these three are one* (NKJV). If you need to determine the origin of a "word" that you hear, research it to see if it lines up with scripture. The enemy's tactics are always to twist or alter scripture as seen in the Garden of Eden (Genesis 2) and when tempting Jesus in the wilderness (Luke 4).

The Holy Spirit Speaks the Word

The role of the Holy Spirit as defined in scripture is:

> *And I will ask the Father, and he will give you another advocate to help you and be with you forever— the Spirit of truth. The world cannot accept him, because it neither sees him nor knows him. But you know him, for he lives with you and will be in you* (John 14:16-17 NIV).

> *When the Spirit of truth comes, he will guide you into all truth. He will not speak on his own but will tell you what he has heard. He will tell you about the future. He will bring me glory by telling you whatever he receives from me. All that belongs to the Father is mine; this is why*

I said, "The Spirit will tell you whatever he receives from me" (John 16:13-15 NLT).

All those led by God's Spirit are God's sons. For you did not receive a spirit of slavery to fall back into fear, but you received the Spirit of adoption, by whom we cry out, "Abba, Father!" The Spirit Himself testifies together with our spirit that we are God's children (Romans 8:14-16 HCSB).

The Holy Spirit will speak truth to you, guide you in truth, and tell you of things to come. He is our Spirit of adoption and communicates to our spirit about our identity, that we are children of God. One way to tell if we are being led by the Holy Spirit is found in Galatians 5. If we are following the Holy Spirit then these passages tell us that the "fruit" of the Spirit is *love, joy, peace, patience, kindness, goodness, faith, gentleness, and self-control.*

We are just seeing a small portion of how Holy Spirit speaks to us. Through the the *logos* and *rhēma* word. I want to encourage you to pray, seek and ask Holy Spirit if there is anything He wants to speak to you. Journal what you hear below:

_____
_____
_____
_____
_____
_____
_____
_____
_____
_____
_____
_____
_____
_____
_____
_____
_____
_____
_____
_____
_____

Week Four - Hearing God

Day Five - Hearing God Through His People

God designed us to live this life in the context of community with other believers. Often, we can get so caught up in our own personal faith walk and the busyness of life that we forget the gift we have been given. As a believer, I have the privilege of walking arm in arm with other believers for the purpose of strengthening my faith, challenging my areas of growth and encouragement.

God has put people in your life to encourage you and challenge you in your faith. It is hard to allow people close enough to speak truth and love into our life. But as we do this, we invite God to work and move in powerful ways.

The way that God encourages and challenges you often comes in the form of prophecy or a prophetic word spoken over you. In the church world, this can sound and even feel a little weird, but it's not. Prophecy is simply speaking words into someone else as the Holy Spirit leads you.

And the coolest part is, **we are all called to prophecy**. It isn't reserved for certain people, places, positions, religions or organizations.

> *Pursue love, and desire spiritual gifts, but especially that you may prophesy. For he who speaks in a tongue does not speak to men but to God, for no one understands him; however, in the spirit he speaks mysteries. But he who prophesies speaks edification and exhortation and comfort to men* (1 Corinthians 14:1-3 NKJV).

We are all called to pursue love and desire spiritual gifts. The purpose of prophecy is clearly laid out. Does it encourage? Does it exhort? Does it comfort?

That's it. The only formula needed. Sometimes, it's a scripture or a word or a whole bunch of words, but that is not the part that matters. What matters is that we are listening to the Holy Spirit speaking as He prompts and saying the things He asks us to say to others.

I can recall a specific prophetic word that was given to me at an event in an envelope. Somebody I did not know wrote a word of prophecy and a scripture for me, not even knowing who it was for. On that evening, I was wrestling with something specific. When I opened the card and read the words written on the inside, it felt like God was speaking directly to my heart and my situation, comforting and encouraging me. Now, God could have spoken those words to me specifically or led me to that scripture in the Word, but instead He chose to use someone else to speak to me.

Let's dive a little deeper into prophecy. Where does prophecy come from? It comes from the Father, Son and Holy Spirit. **The purpose of prophecy is hearing God for yourself and others.** The fruit of prophecy is encouragement, edification and exhortation in the body of Christ. The benefit is for others not just ourselves.

When you receive a word, it stays in you, and you often get to release it to someone else. Because the Word is alive and active, when God speaks His words to you through someone else, it awakens something inside of you. It usually confirms something you were already feeling, reminds you of something He has already told you or ignites something brand new inside of you.

In the body of Christ there are many expressions of prophecy, and we have seen people give incredible words from a platform, but this gift is just as powerful in a one-on-one conversation or written encouragement. Some of my most life-altering moments came in the form of a simple encouraging card in the mail that was divinely timed and altered the way I walked with God the rest of my life.

We can give encouraging words that have a major impact on the lives of others. We must be willing to give and receive words of prophecy with love, grace and honor.

Divine Timing

We have been studying about the Word of God and ways God speaks to us as sons and daughters of God. What makes all this so mind blowing to me is that GOD WANTS TO TALK TO US! Do you really receive that for you? He desires to reveal Himself to you through so many glorious and powerful expressions of His love.

Revelation and prophecy are beautifully intertwined. Simply stated, prophecy is a type of revelation and hearing the voice of God, both for yourself and others. You don't have to be a perfect person nor a super hero to hear from God, but you will have to take a leap of faith and risk sharing it with others.

If I could teach one thing about prophecy and revelation, it would be this: **God speaks in order to encourage, exhort, discipline, direct, reveal, and comfort His children**. It's simple when you think about it. He loves us! He really is a good good Father.

Let's read through a few scriptures. (We challenge you to find these in YOUR Bible, highlight them and write beside them as He speaks through His Word).

> *And it shall come to pass in the last days, says God, that I will pour out of My Spirit on all flesh; your sons and your daughters shall prophesy, your young men shall see visions, your old men shall dream dreams. And on My menservants and on My maidservants, I will pour out My Spirit in those days; and they shall prophesy (Acts 2:17-18 NKJV).*

> *Having then gifts differing according to the grace that is given to us, let us use them: If prophecy, let us prophesy in proportion to our faith (Romans 12:6 NKJV).*

> *Pursue love, and desire spiritual gifts, but especially that you may prophesy. For he who speaks in a tongue does not speak to men but to God, for no one understands him; however, in the spirit he speaks mysteries. But he who prophesies speaks edification and exhortation and comfort to men (1 Corinthians 14:1-3 NKJV).*

Earlier, I said revelation and prophecy are beautifully intertwined together, so let's do some spiritual math (I usually hate math but not today).

Prayer plus the **Word of God** multiplied by the **Holy Spirit equals heaven touching earth through you**. This spiritual math must not be done on paper but in faith.

PRAYER + WORD x HOLY SPIRIT = POWER

Have you ever experienced receiving a prophetic word from someone before?

_____

_____

_____

_____

_____

Has God ever revealed something about someone to you that would encourage or comfort them?

_____
_____
_____
_____
_____
_____
_____
_____

How would you like to get a word from God right now? Pray, ask Him for a word and write it down.

Prayer: Father God I want to thank you for loving me. I receive your love right now. Jesus, thank you for what you accomplished on the cross for me. I declare that I am the righteousness of God through Jesus Christ. Holy Spirit will you show me your heart for me through words, pictures or through my surroundings.

Now just receive and believe what God says to you and journal what you heard:

_____
_____
_____
_____
_____
_____
_____
_____

Now I want you to think of your best friend, spouse or child. I want you to repeat the same prayer above, but this time, I want you to ask the Holy Spirit to give you an encouraging word for them. Write it down in the space below.

_____
_____
_____
_____
_____
_____
_____
_____

There is a wide range of ways you can encourage others

- **A written note put in the mail with encouragement or a scripture for someone.** We have gotten away from the practice of handwritten mail. There is so much power in the written word.

- **A specific word that comes to mind when you think of someone** Example: Marc is an encourager. It is who he is, but when that comes to my mind, it might be at the exact time that he needs to be reminded of who he is! We should not assume that leaders and the people around us are being encouraged. Your words are powerful.

- **A scripture** Sometimes when you're reading in the Bible someone comes to mind as you're reading a scripture. At times, all we are supposed to do is share that scripture with them and allow them to seek the Holy Spirit for revelation and understanding.

- **A phone call instead of a text just to hear someone's voice.** You can tell a lot by the tone of someone's voice and Holy Spirit will give you the opportunity to speak into their lives. One of the most powerful things you can do is just ask them if you can pray for them. Then pray for them.

- **A small token gift that reminds you of them.** Sometimes when you are out and about you run across something that makes you think of someone specific. Grab that item and make it a point to deliver it personally or drop it off in a creative way.

Our challenge to you is to intentionally complete one of these fun ways to encourage someone. I promise it will be a blessing to you and them.

Week Four - Hearing God

Day Six - Resting in His Creation

Being able to hear and recognize the voice of God is one of our greatest blessings. As a believer, I must practice being still and getting alone with Him. One of my favorite invitations from Jesus is when He says to His disciples, "come away with me."

> *The apostles gathered around Jesus and reported to him all they had done and taught. Then, because so many people were coming and going that they did not even have a chance to eat, he said to them, "Come with me by yourselves to a quiet place and get some rest." So they went away by themselves in a boat to a solitary place* (Mark 6:30-32 NIV).

This is our invitation from our Heavenly Father today. Just as He taught the disciples, we get to create a habit of getting away from it all for a minute, an hour or even a day to just be with Him.

As a ministry, we host an event called Fully Alive for men and women to take a few days to press into what God wants to say, to discover the lies they've been believing that hold them in bondage, and to find healing and release from those lies so they can run in freedom toward God in their everyday lives. One part of this amazing weekend is intentional time set aside to respond to Jesus's invitation to "come away" with Him. We like to refer to this as our "**go to the woods**" time. As impactful as this time is on a weekend event, it's even more powerful in the midst of our normal, everyday, hectic lives.

Today we are challenging you to **go to the woods**. Take some time to get still and rest in His creation. It may be your own backyard or sitting by a pool or water fountain downtown. You may plan an excursion to a local park or go hike at a nearby state park. The location doesn't matter as much as the heart to step out of your comfort zone and routine and jump into some one-on-one time with the Lord surrounded by the sights and sounds of nature. It's incredible how He uses His creation to speak to us.

As you go, take your Bible and a notepad or journal, a pen and a readied heart.

Ask the Holy Spirit where you should go, if you should walk or where you should sit. It may sound or seem silly, but it's all just a part of practicing hearing God and interacting with Him. Remember, God desires a relationship with you.

Journal what you see, hear and experience. Those random thoughts that pop up in your head are usually Holy Spirit sparking something in you.

Sometimes we just need to lie down and rest in Him. The simple act of lying down in the grass and allowing Him to hold you in the palm of His hand (His creation) can breathe life and peace into you. The weather, the trees, the birds or bugs, they're all a part of experiencing God.

When the created walk among creation, the Creator shows up every time. In the beginning, Genesis tells us God loved walking though the garden in the cool of the evening with Adam and Eve. He longs to walk with you as well. Take time to notice everything.

As you spend time with Him, here are a few questions you can pray through. Pick one, all or none. These are just here as a guide.

Father, what's on your heart and mind today?

What do you want to say to me?

What do you want me to see through this one-of-a-kind experience in creation today?

Do you really love me?

What do you see when you see me?

Share what you hear below:

_____
_____
_____
_____

Grace, Love and Holy Spirit

The Cross

God sent His son to live in a fallen world and die a horrific death to demonstrate His perfect love and to build our imperfect faith.

Week Five - The Cross

Day One - The Story of the Cross

It is by His stripes we are healed. Because of the cross, we are able to live in community and unity with the Father, Son and Holy Spirit.

Sometimes we can hear the story of the cross, and it doesn't carry the weight it deserves in our lives. It's not just a great story for Easter. It is an important piece of our story every day we are alive on this earth.

Grab your Bible and take some time to read through John chapter 19.

Reflect on what happened to Jesus leading up to and during His crucifixion.

Can you visualize being there and watching this happen? Read through this passage again a second time and journal your thoughts and feelings.

_____
_____
_____
_____
_____
_____
_____
_____
_____
_____
_____
_____
_____
_____
_____
_____

_____
_____
_____
_____
_____
_____
_____
_____
_____
_____
_____
_____
_____
_____
_____
_____
_____
_____
_____
_____
_____
_____
_____
_____
_____
_____

Keep this on the forefront of your mind. It can be easy for us to live our busy lives without acknowledging the cross. Ask the Lord to help you to be mindful of the cross as you go throughout your day today.

This week we will memorize 1 Peter 2:24. Jot this verse down and keep it posted where you can see it. Every time you read this verse thank Him for the healing we have through Him.

> _He himself bore our sins in His body on a tree, that we might die to sin and live to righteousness. By his wounds you have been healed_ (1 Peter 2:24 ESV).

Week Five - The Cross

Day Two - Salvation Through the Cross

In week one, we read about Jesus being the Word that dwelt among us -- the perfect, spotless Lamb of God who would take away the sins of the world and the life-giving gift from God to the world. **God's Word is full of scriptures that hold promises and truths that we can embrace and live by.** So many scriptures tell us exactly what to do as we read them.

While studying a few years ago, it was a huge revelation when I discovered how many scriptures clearly lay out God's part and my part. Let's break this down. God's Word is full of specific promises and exhortations. Let's take a well-known scripture and unpack this concept.

> *Therefore, do not worry, saying, "What shall we eat?" or "What shall we drink?" or "What shall we wear?" For after all these things the Gentiles seek. For your heavenly Father knows that you need all these things. But seek first the kingdom of God and His righteousness, and all these things shall be added to you* (Matthew 6:32-33 NIV).

Seek first the Kingdom of God and everything else will be added unto you. Our part is to seek first the Kingdom of God. His part is everything else. We do not have to worry about *what we will eat, drink or wear*. He wants to take care of all of that as we seek Him.

Now regarding Jesus and salvation, let us apply this concept again, my part and His part. In your Bible read John 3:16 and as you read through it, circle God's part and underline your part.

- God loved- Who does God love?
- God gave- What did He give?
- We believe-What are we believing?
- We receive-What will we receive?

The Cross is God's Love Demonstrated for Us

We have established the relationship between God and Jesus. God sent His son to live and die for you and me. The magnitude of this love relationship is overwhelming and beyond comprehension. If you have children, it is hard to look at them and even consider allowing what happened to Jesus to happen to your child. But Jesus was the way, the truth and the life. The only way for us to get to God was through Him (Jesus), and He knew it.

The sweetest part is that He (Jesus) wanted us to be with Him and His Father (God) in heaven so badly that He (Jesus) was willing to do the hardest thing He'd ever have to do.

> *Fixing our eyes on Jesus, the pioneer and perfecter of faith. For the joy set before him he endured the cross, scorning its shame, and sat down at the right hand of the throne of God. (Hebrews 12:2 NIV).*

Read the passage in Romans and see how salvation becomes ours.

> *If you declare with your mouth, "Jesus is Lord," and believe in your heart that God raised him from the dead, you will be saved. For it is with your heart that you believe and are justified, and it is with your mouth that you profess your faith and are saved (Romans 10:9-10 NIV).*

Our part is to confess with our mouth that Jesus is Lord and believe in our hearts God raised Him from the dead, and if we do those two simple things, we will be saved. Salvation is a matter of the heart. The heart is where we believe what we believe. We call on the name of the Lord because we believe, and because we believe we are saved.

Read Romans 10:9-10 again. In your own words, what are we believing in?

_____
_____
_____
_____
_____

The Cross Made a Way for Me

Has there been a time in your life where you have chosen to believe in Jesus, confessed Him as Lord of your life, chosen to trust God's plan of redemption for yourself and surrendered your life to Jesus? If not, we've written a letter in the back of this book just for you. Turn to page 175.

If you have confessed Jesus as Lord of your life, write out your salvation story as if you had just a few minutes to share it with someone. After journaling your salvation story, pray over it, thanking Him for your gift of salvation and asking Him for opportunities to share your story with others as He opens the door.

Who was I before salvation?

_____
_____
_____
_____
_____
_____
_____
_____
_____
_____
_____

What did my salvation look like?

_____
_____
_____
_____
_____
_____
_____
_____
_____
_____
_____

How did my life change because of my salvation?

_____
_____
_____
_____

_____
_____
_____
_____
_____
_____
_____
_____

When the power of the cross and your story collide, we have the opportunity to share the cross and our testimony with others, and it has transforming power.

As a team, we are surprised to find out how many haven't learned how to share our story. We've kept it a private matter, but the power of our story comes as we share it with others. Our lives were changed because of the cross, and we get to offer that same life-changing power to those we encounter. Someone may be waiting to hear the powerful truth that only you can share from your vantage point through your experience.

Week Five - The Cross

Day Three - Grace and the Cross

The grace we experience daily came at a cost. The cross is God's love displayed for mankind through real sacrifice. It says in Romans 8:3 that what the law was powerless to do, God did by sending His Son as a sin offering, and so He condemned sin rather than man!

The Gift of Salvation

Salvation is not something we achieve but a gift we receive. We cannot work hard enough or perform well enough to earn the approval of God because we already have it. You cannot earn something you already possess.

Birthdays are for celebrating! We all have a birthday. Whether you love celebrating your birthday or dread it, one truth remains: you did nothing to earn your birthday. It is a day where you are celebrated usually with cake and gifts or cards. You do not work hard all year for your birthday gift. There is no master list of everything great you have done or demerits for the things you have done wrong that settle up to the sum total of how well you are or are not celebrated on your birthday.

It seems foolish, but this is exactly what we do. We have such a hard time receiving something that has been freely given to us.

Because of the Cross We are Made Alive in Christ

We are not saved by works or anything we can do. No one deserves the credit but Jesus. His love alone gives life and we live loved because of His grace and kindness.

As for you, you were dead in your transgressions and sins, in which you used to live when you followed the ways of this world and of the ruler of the kingdom of the air, the spirit who is now at work in those who are disobedient. All of us also lived among them at one time, gratifying the cravings of our flesh and following its desires and thoughts. Like the rest, we were by nature deserving of wrath. But because of his great love for us, God, who is rich in mercy, made us alive with Christ even when we were dead in transgressions—it is by grace you have been saved. And God raised us up with Christ and seated us with him in the heavenly realms in Christ Jesus, in order that in the coming ages he might show the incomparable riches of his grace, expressed in his kindness to us in Christ Jesus. For it is by grace you have been saved, through faith—and this is not from yourselves, it is the gift of God— not by works, so that no one can boast. For we are God's handiwork, created in Christ Jesus to do good works, which God prepared in advance for us to do (Ephesians 2:1-10 NIV).

This passage clearly tells us that we are saved by _____.

If we are saved by grace, why do we get caught up trying to perform to gain His love and approval and to earn our gift of salvation? Take a few minutes and ask Holy Spirit if there are any areas of your life where you are trying to earn His love or are working for the free gift of salvation. Write out what He reveals.

_____
_____
_____
_____
_____
_____
_____
_____

Because our salvation does not come from what we do but who we are, or better, whose we are, we can take a deep breath and lean into His love and grace. Sometimes this is the hardest thing for us to do as believers. **We tend to get so busy trying to do for God that we miss what He has done or is doing for us.**

As you walk through your day today, I encourage you to ask yourself if you are working for His love or resting in and receiving His love. Working for his love feels like... WORK. Walking in His love feels like a gift or a blessing, and it is life-giving.

Nothing Can Separate Us from God's Love

God sent His son to live in a fallen world and die a horrific death to demonstrate His perfect love and to build our imperfect faith. Read the passage below and underline the word <u>NOTHING</u> every time it is mentioned.

> *What shall we say about such wonderful things as these? If God is for us, who can ever be against us? Since He did not spare even His own Son but gave Him up for us all, won't He also give us everything else? Who dares accuse us whom God has chosen for His own? No one—for God Himself has given us right standing with Himself. Who then will condemn us? No one—for Christ Jesus died for us and was raised to life for us, and He is sitting in the place of honor at God's right hand, pleading for us. Can anything ever separate us from Christ's love? Does it mean He no longer loves us if we have trouble or calamity, or are persecuted, or hungry, or destitute, or in danger, or threatened with death? (As the Scriptures say, "For your sake we are killed every day; we are being slaughtered like sheep.") No, despite all these things, overwhelming victory is ours through Christ, who loved us. And I am convinced that nothing can ever separate us from God's love. Neither death nor life, neither angels nor demons, neither our fears for today nor our worries about tomorrow—not even the powers of hell can separate us from God's love. No power in the sky above or in the earth below—indeed, nothing in all creation will ever be able to separate us from the love of God that is revealed in Christ Jesus our Lord* (Romans 8:31-39 NLT).

<u>NOTHING</u> can separate us from the love of God. Not our actions or attitudes or the actions of others can move us away from His love. This miraculous, amazing love was lived out for everyone to see on the cross **through Christ**. The perfect love of God was made available to all of us **through the cross**. We can grab hold of the inheritance that is rightfully ours **through faith**. Remember, the righteous live by faith.

Read Hebrews chapter 11:1-30 in your Bible and circle the word faith every time you see it.

We are going to face faith challenges daily. Opportunities to embrace the encouraging love of the Father will be a daily choice as well. Our actions reflect how we choose daily to discern and deal with the challenges and overcome them with truth.

Ask the Holy Spirit to give you revelation about what was truly accomplished through the cross. He guides us into all truth (John 16:13). The cross is the unchangeable and unshakable covenant between God and us.

For many, the image of the cross is a bloody, historical scene, but the truth be told, the cross is where GRACE (JESUS) delivers the ultimate knockout punch to the devil and what he did in the garden when he deceived mankind. God is love, but one thing we must understand is that His love is not wimpy or weak! The Bible tells us that perfect love drives out fear (1 John 4:18). Jesus, the ultimate love warrior, showed up and kicked the devil's tail that day. Once you grasp that revelation and reality, you become empowered with the same power Jesus walked in.

What's your BY FAITH story going to be? How will you be remembered for generations to come? Take a few minutes and write your own version of Hebrews 11, your BY FAITH Declaration. We've included our Declaration as a sample to get you started.

OUR BY FAITH DECLARATION:
BY FAITH the elevateHim Team believes that God has positioned and empowered us to write a resource that can equip, impact and change lives by laying a foundation rooted in the Word. BY FAITH we invested our five kingdom currencies (time, talent, treasure, touch and words) into the Sons and Daughters of God. BY FAITH we chose to write collaboratively but anonymously as we blended genders, backgrounds, styles, and personalities believing the result would be a resource that allows people to hear and connect with God, instead of individuals.

YOUR BY FAITH DECLARATION:
BY FAITH _____

_____

_____

_____

_____

_____

_____

_____

_____

_____

_____

_____

_____

_____

Week Five - The Cross

Day Four - The Finished Work of the Cross

Jesus did not rescue you because you have a purpose. He rescued you because He loves you! **His love is the purpose, and the cross is both natural and supernatural proof of His love for you.** When we understand the power of the cross, we are embracing the depth of His great love for us.

Letting Go of the Past

Many times, the best way to move forward with purpose is to forgive ourselves for the past. Before the cross, we were bound by law. Jesus came not to abolish the law but to fulfill the law.

> *Do not think that I have come to abolish the Law or the Prophets; I have not come to abolish them but to fulfill them. For truly, I say to you, until heaven and earth pass away, not an iota, not a dot, will pass from the Law until all is accomplished. Therefore, whoever relaxes one of the least of these commandments and teaches others to do the same will be called least in the kingdom of heaven, but whoever does them and teaches them will be called great in the kingdom of heaven. For I tell you, unless your righteousness exceeds that of the scribes and Pharisees, you will never enter the kingdom of heaven* (Matthew 5:17-20 ESV).

The law in and of itself was created because there was no Holy Spirit governing God's people. In the Old Testament the Israelites asked for and established their governing laws. Jesus fulfilled the law when He spoke His final words on the cross that it was finished.

It Is Finished

> *After this, Jesus, knowing that all things were now accomplished, that*

the Scripture might be fulfilled, said, "I thirst!" Now a vessel full of sour wine was sitting there; and they filled a sponge with sour wine, put it on hyssop, and put it to His mouth. So, when Jesus had received the sour wine, He said, "It is finished!" And bowing His head, He gave up His spirit (John 19:28-30 KJV).

The fulfilled work of the cross means there is no more work for us to do to obtain salvation. He has accomplished that for us on the cross.

For Christ's love compels us; because we are convinced that one died for all, and therefore all died. And He died for all, that those who live should no longer live for themselves but for him who died for them and was raised again. So, from now on we regard no one from a worldly point of view. Though we once regarded Christ in this way, we do so no longer. Therefore, if anyone is in Christ, the new creation has come: The old has gone, the new is here! All this is from God, who reconciled us to Himself through Christ and gave us the ministry of reconciliation: that God was reconciling the world to himself in Christ, not counting people's sins against them. And He has committed to us the message of reconciliation. We are therefore Christ's ambassadors, as though God were making his appeal through us. We implore you on Christ's behalf: Be reconciled to God. God made Him who had no sin to be sin for us, so that in Him we might become the righteousness of God (2 Corinthians 5:14-21 NIV).

He became sin so that we could become the righteousness of God. Let that soak in for a minute. What does it mean to be the righteousness of God?

_____

_____

_____

_____

Being the righteousness of God means I stop working, striving and trying to prove myself. Jesus did all the heavy lifting and now I can rest in His love and grace.

When you surrendered your life to Christ and accepted the gift of salvation, your sins from yesterday, today and tomorrow were reconciled. He paid the price for them all. We can get caught up in the idea that He has forgiven our past sins but has yet to forgive us for any new sin. We get to choose to live by faith in the One who was sent for us.

Faith or Works of the Law

O foolish Galatians! Who has bewitched you? It was before your eyes that Jesus Christ was publicly portrayed as crucified. Let me ask you only this: Did you receive the Spirit by the works of the law or by hearing with faith? Are you so foolish? Having begun by the Spirit, are you now being perfected by the flesh? Did you suffer so many things in vain—if indeed it was in vain? Does He who supplies Spirit to you and works miracles among you do so by the works of the law, or hearing with faith- Just as Abraham "believed God, and it was counted to him as righteousness"? Know then that it is those of faith who are the sons of Abraham. And the scripture, foreseeing that God would justify the Gentiles by faith, preached the gospel in beforehand to Abraham, saying "In you shall all the nations be blessed." So then, those who are of faith are blessed along with Abraham, the man of faith. For all who rely on the works of the law are under a curse; for it is written: "Cursed be everyone who does not abide by all things written in the Book of the Law, and do them." Now it is evident that no one is justified before God by the law, for "the righteous will live by faith." But the law is not of faith, rather "The one who does them shall live by them." Christ redeemed us from the curse of the law by becoming a curse for us, for it is written: "Cursed is everyone who is hanged on a tree"- so that in Christ Jesus the blessing of Abraham might come to the Gentiles, so that we might receive the promised Spirit through faith (Galatians 3:1-14 NIV).

What does this passage say we receive by faith through Jesus?_____

How will we achieve this promised blessing? _____

Sometimes it's easy to get sucked back into a false belief that we have to earn our salvation by how we live our lives. The truth is, because we love Him, we obey the truths in His Word and the things He speaks to our spirit. We do not obey to earn His love or our salvation, but we obey because we are saved. We know His great, inexplicable and undeserving love for us.

While we were sinners, Christ died for us. You are no longer a sinner but the righteousness of God through Christ Jesus.

Peace and Hope

Therefore, since we have been justified through faith, we have peace with God through our Lord Jesus Christ, through whom we have gained access by faith into this grace in which we now stand. And we boast in the hope of the glory of God. Not only so, but we also glory in our sufferings, because we know that suffering produces perseverance; perseverance, character; and character, hope. And hope does not put us to shame, because God's love has been poured out into our hearts through the Holy Spirit, who has been given to us. You see, at just the right time, when we were still powerless, Christ died for the ungodly. Very rarely will anyone die for a righteous person, though for a good person someone might possibly dare to die. But God demonstrates his own love for us in this: While we were still sinners, Christ died for us. Since we have now been justified by His blood, how much more shall we be saved from God's wrath through Him! For if, while we were God's enemies, we were reconciled to Him through the death of his Son, how much more, having been reconciled, shall we be saved through His life! Not only is this so, but we also boast in God through our Lord Jesus Christ, through whom we have now received reconciliation (Romans 5:1-10 NIV).

This week we have unpacked the power and necessity of the cross. Ultimately, we can rest in this truth. Take the time to write a letter to God thanking Him for the cross and sharing with Him what it means to you personally.

_____
_____
_____
_____
_____
_____
_____
_____
_____
_____
_____
_____

Week Five - The Cross

Day Five - The Resurrection Power

We've talked this week about all the work that was done on the cross. What happened three days after the cross was equally as important, the resurrection. **We can rest in the eternal display of God's love for us through the defining moment of the resurrection.**

Grab your Bible and read Matthew 27:57-28:20. As you read the account of the burial and resurrection jot down what stands out to you.

One of the greatest truths about this moment in time was that no one on this earth had anything to do with the resurrection. No man had the strength or power to open the grave, rolling away the stone. The discovery of the empty tomb happened after God worked in His mighty power to raise Jesus from the dead.

The resurrection isn't just an event that happened a long time ago. It is THE EVENT that changed the course of history for you and me! The daily choice is ours to live in constant communion with the one who demonstrated His unmatched power for the world to see or choose to live like it didn't happen.

Through the resurrection God's ultimate Love and Grace were on display for the world to see, only not everyone could see. Jesus appeared to many and those individuals shared with the people they encountered but what about the people who never got to hear the incredible news about the miracle of the resurrection? That's why He told His disciples to go and make disciples of every nation. We get to share the incredible story with everyone!

The Joy that Comes from His Love

The passage you read a minute ago in Matthew said Mary was "afraid yet filled with joy" and ran to tell the disciples. Let's stop right there for a minute. When was the last time you were so excited about something that you ran to tell someone about it? Sometimes I run to grab my phone and call someone, but the physical representation of running to tell everyone what she discovered just ignites a feeling of passion, purpose and tenacity.

Are we living our lives with the same excitement Mary did after she discovered the empty tomb and Jesus appeared to her in such a sweet and personal encounter? Are we living like the disciples who were given specific instructions by Jesus himself after He had risen from the dead, before He ascended to His rightful place at the right hand of the Father?

This was an epic life-changing event for Mary, the disciples, and those who heard, saw and believed. It is an epic life-changing event for you and me also.

When was the last time you felt amazed by the presence of God and filled with joy?

_____

_____

_____

_____

_____

_____

_____

_____

_____

_____

_____

What was the last thing that happened to you that you were so excited to share with someone else?

_____

_____

_____

_____

_____

_____

_____

_____

_____

When was the last time you were this excited about something God revealed or spoke to you that you "ran to tell" someone?

_____
_____
_____
_____
_____
_____
_____
_____
_____
_____

God Demonstrates His Power

The Spirit of God, who raised Jesus from the dead, lives in you. And just as God raised Christ Jesus from the dead, he will give life to your mortal bodies by this same Spirit living within you (Romans 8:11 NLT).

The same power displayed through the resurrection is now at work in you. We can now rest in this powerful truth.

The resurrection illustrated a few things for us:
- Redemption is ours!
- God demonstrated His power!
- Jesus demolished sin and a debt we could not pay!
- Jesus' work was finished!
- The stone was rolled away, and Jesus wasn't there!
- He is now sitting in his rightful place as the King of Glory!
- We have a promise to meet Him face to face in Heaven!

The Choice is Ours

Today we get to choose to live like we believe that the same power demonstrated through the resurrection of Jesus is alive in us. We carry a responsibility to share the truth we know and the relationship we have with Him to a lost and dying world.

Here's just one of the powerful truths Jesus shared with His disciples:

"As the Father has loved me, so have I loved you. Now remain in My love. If you keep my commands, you will remain in My love, just as I

have kept my Father's commands and remain in His love. I have told you this so that My joy may be in you and that your joy may be complete. My command is this: Love each other as I have loved you. Greater love has no one than this: to lay down one's life for one's friends. You are my friends if you do what I command. I no longer call you servants, because a servant does not know his master's business. Instead, I have called you friends, for everything that I learned from My Father I have made known to you. You did not choose me, but I chose you and appointed you so that you might go and bear fruit—fruit that will last—and so that whatever you ask in my name the Father will give you. This is my command: Love each other (John 15:9-17 NIV).

As we wrap up this week, we can walk in the power of the resurrection every day. We can share about His mighty power at work in us and the world around us with everyone we see. We want to be mindful, in a constant state of awareness. When we grow tired, get busy or sway to a position of indifference, we want to press in, look for God's mighty hand at work and return to our most important mission; receiving and believing His grace, love and Holy Spirit.

Take a moment in prayer asking the Father to illuminate His power at work in you and in your life. Take a minute and write out, as if you were sharing with a friend, what God is doing in your life, how you've seen Him show up, speak truth to you, and where you've experienced His power at work in and through you.

Week Five - The Cross

Day Six - Resting in the Cross

We were created for communion with the Father. What Jesus did on the cross changed our lives forever. What Jesus did before the cross set the example for all to follow. When He gathered His disciples in the upper room, and He broke the bread and passed the cup, it was symbolic of what was coming. We get to create a habit of resting in the cross -- the body that was broken for us, the blood that was shed for us, and the resurrected King.

Read the story of the Last Supper. It is found in Matthew 26:17-30, Luke 22: 7-39, and Mark 14: 12-26. Pick one of these passages and read through it.

Growing up in church, I remember the phrase "*...do this in remembrance of me...*" as we took communion. I understood the "*remember*" part but what I was remembering was a little off. We may have been taught to remember the death, broken body and shed blood, but because of our love relationship with God through Jesus, we not only remember what He did but celebrate what He is still doing. The last supper was Jesus' covenant with His disciples, and we choose daily to make a covenant with Jesus. Remembrance means to recall the memory of the event. Yes, we remember the brutal, bloody death on the cross, but do you ever stop to think of Him seated at the right hand of the Father fully empowered?

We have a hard time understanding or relating to the word 'covenant.' In Jesus' time everyone knew what a blood covenant meant. When Jesus broke the bread that represented His body and passed the cup that represented His blood, He was entering into covenant with His disciples. The Old Testament covenant, was called a blessing and a curse, demanded unrighteous man to fulfill righteous law. Jesus' new covenant doesn't focus at all on what we can do, but puts the full weight and glory on Jesus' ability to fulfill His covenant to His people.

His covenant to His people:

- I will provide for all of your needs (Philippians 4:19).
- I will protect you from your enemies (2 Thessalonians 3:3).
- I will heal your people and your land (2 Chronicles 7:14).
- I will redeem what the enemy has stolen (Deuteronomy 30:3-5).
- I will restore your relationship to the Father and destroy the barrier that keeps you from having full access to Him (Ephesians 3:12).

When we choose to take communion, we need to remember Jesus' sacrifice on the cross, but more importantly, that He completely finished the work, fulfilled the laws and abolished the rules supremely. **Because of His covenant with us, we can go boldly before the throne of God that is full of grace and love for His sons and daughters**. In the old covenant, you had to "do" something to get something. In the new covenant, He gave it all to us.

Communion is not a commemoration or a ritual; it's a celebration! It is an opportunity to acknowledge what He has done, is still doing and will continue to do for us because of the cross.

Let's practice resting through Communion together. Grab something solid an something liquid -- bread, cracker, protein bar and a drink, whatever you have around you is perfect. We use tortilla chips and soda around the table at a Mexican restaurant. It's not about the elements, it's about the heart. We've created a simple guide to Communion for you on pages 178-179.

Take a few minutes to remember (recall the terms of agreement) the covenant that Jesus made with you and for you.

How have you seen God:

- Protect   _____

- Provide   _____

- Heal   _____

- Redeem   _____

- Restore   _____

Sin and the Real Enemy

Fear is the enemy's prophetic lie over your life. Faith is God's prophetic truth ordained for your life!

Week Six - Sin and the Real Enemy

Day One - Sin is Missing the Mark

Sin is a sensitive subject that believers either have a hard time talking about or over commercialize and objectify. The truth is, the temptation of sin is a part of everyday life for believers and non-believers the same.

Sin is sin

One of the words for sin in the New Testament is the Greek word *hamartia*, which originally meant "to miss the mark."

God's will and God's design for us is to live in perfect unity with Him. Sin is what stands in the way and breaks the unity between God and us if we let it. But the great thing is, Jesus died for our sin so that it no longer separates us from Him.

Sin is, simply put, when we miss the mark. The mark is Christ-likeness.

Have you ever shot a compound bow or watched someone shoot one? A few years ago, at a 3D archery tournament, I watched archers young and old all working with the same goal in mind: to hit the mark, or the bullseye on the designated target. The mark was clearly laid out, easy to see and theirs for the taking. Each archer would sight their bow, point toward the mark and shoot. Many would miss, some would get close, and a few would hit it every time.

Our faith walk is similar. It's pretty easy to miss the mark. We can miss it consistently and repeatedly, occasionally or rarely, but in the Kingdom equation, how often we hit or miss the mark doesn't rank us or earn us trophies like in an archery tournament.

Judgment has no part in God's heart. A wrong belief system can cause you to miss the mark every time. A right belief system allows you to be empowered by Christ.

Remember, God is love.

As we dive into this week, we will talk about sin, how to identify it, the enemy's tactics against us and the beautiful exchange God offered through Jesus.

When you hear the word sin, what comes to mind? Write your thoughts below.

_____

_____

_____

_____

_____

_____

_____

_____

_____

_____

If sin is simply missing the mark, do you spend more time and energy worried about your sin (where you're missing it) or focusing on the target (Christ-likeness, grace, truth and mercy)? Why do you think that is?

_____

_____

_____

_____

_____

_____

_____

_____

_____

_____

Take a few minutes to pray and ask the Lord to help you shift your focus from your sin to His love and nature as you learn to live in His grace, truth, and love.

This week we will memorize Romans 6:14 together.

> *For sin will have no dominion over you, since you are not under law but under grace. (Romans 6:14 ESV)*

Week Six - Sin and the Real Enemy

Day Two - Sin isn't the Focus

Have you ever heard one of the below statements?

"Keep your eyes on the prize."
"Don't get distracted from what you really want."
"Focus on your purpose."
"Keep your eyes on the ball."
"Keep the main thing the main thing."

At a Garden Party in 1994, William Gates II (the father of Microsoft founder Bill Gates III) posed this question to his distinguished dinner guests, who were at the time the two richest men in America: "What factor do you feel was most important to getting where you've gotten in life?"

Both guests, Warren Buffett and Bill Gates, replied "**focus**".

A primary task of leadership is to direct attention. To achieve this, leaders must learn to focus their own attention and direct others to focus on their goal. Every parent, teacher, coach, pastor, and leader repeatedly communicates the importance of "FOCUS."

Be careful what leader you are following because what they focus on becomes your focus. The enemy is a leadership guru of deception and distraction. He loves hate. Yes, that's right. He loves hate, lies and deception because he is the very opposite of our loving Father God. The devil has laser focus on a very clever plan… distracting you. The devil wants your focus so you will follow his lead.

Sin and the Curse

So the Lord God said to the serpent, "Because you have done this, Cursed are you above all livestock and all wild animals! You will crawl on your belly and you will eat dust all the days of your life" (Genesis 3:14 NIV).

God clearly curses satan for deceiving Adam and Eve. I'm not sure what satan looked like before he got body-slammed by God, but one thing is clear, he is now forced to live in the dust.

Now the devil's slithery plan is to get you focused on the dust and dirt of your journey. To eat dust is to feed and focus on your shortcomings and lack until you constantly feel like you have to wash up, or worse, you just give up. We become so sin conscious that the devil has moved our whole focus to dust, sin, and failures. The devil wants you to focus on your sins and create hopelessness. He can't blind you with his darkness, but he can blind you with your dust and failures. He has been using this tactic for years, and we have been partnering with this dust-viper.

Join me in reading this small scripture out loud:

> *Let your eyes look directly forward, and your gaze be straight before you* (Proverbs 4:25 ESV).

The Holy Spirit desires to lead us into all truth, grace, and love. In the previous passage, we see that as sons and daughters of God, we are to fix our eyes straight ahead. So what does that mean exactly? Fix and focus your eyes on Jesus not the dust. Jesus came to set you free so that you can focus on Him, not your sin. **Sin isn't the main thing to focus on, but rather He who overcame ALL SIN!**

> *Therefore, since we are surrounded by such a great cloud of witnesses, let us throw off everything that hinders and the sin that so easily entangles. And let us run with perseverance the race marked out for us, fixing (FOCUS) our eyes on Jesus, the pioneer and perfecter of our faith. For the joy set before him he endured the cross, scorning its shame, and sat down at the right hand of the throne of God. Consider him who endured such opposition from sinners, so that you will not grow weary and lose heart* (Hebrews 12:1-3 NIV emphasis added).

Focusing on the sin (dust) never sets you free. As a matter of fact, it causes you to grow weary and lose heart. We have been given the freedom to FOCUS our minds on something much more powerful than sin.

> *Finally, brothers, whatever is true, whatever is honorable, whatever is just, whatever is pure, whatever is lovely, whatever is commendable, if*

there is any excellence, if there is anything worthy of praise, think about these things (Philippians 4:8 ESV).

Today I want you to start to make the shift. I don't want you to write down one thing that has to do with how you are missing the mark. I want you to make a list based on Philippians 4:8. Write below ways that you can FOCUS on these things.

Honorable:

_____
_____
_____

Pure:

_____
_____
_____

Lovely:

_____
_____
_____

Commendable:

_____
_____
_____

Now, make a second list of things that you can worship and thank Jesus for today:

- _____ - _____

- _____ - _____

- _____ - _____

- _____ - _____

Week Six - Sin and the Real Enemy

Day Three - We are Already Forgiven

Yesterday we learned that partnering with the dust-viper only keeps us focusing on our sin and shortcomings. Satan plans to never let you forget about your past and your failures. Our goal is to break the pattern of sin-focused believers. We are sick and tired of seeing our brothers and sisters feeling sick and tired. In fact, we want to turn your focus away from sin and turn it toward the unmerited favor of Jesus Christ.

He Remembers No Longer

It's time to stop our constant obsessing over our sin. It's time to stop our incessant prayers of "I'm just a lowly sinner." It's time to stop our feelings of guilt and shame over something that God no longer remembers. Do you hear me? He no longer chooses to remember your sin (Psalm 103:11-12). He has chosen to forget your sins, and yet you continue to agonize and fret over them. Think about the madness of that!

> "*For I will forgive their wickedness and will remember their sins no more*" (Hebrews 8:12 NIV).

Brothers and sisters, stop this insanity and begin to view yourself as God sees you. He doesn't call you sinner; He calls you righteous! He doesn't call you a failure; He calls you perfect! He doesn't call you worthless; He calls you His treasure! As Paul wrote to the Corinthians, all the promises of God are 'yes' through Jesus Christ. It's time to align your thoughts and your beliefs with who He says you are because if you don't, you'll spend the rest of your life in the dust, never seeing all that you had been given and all that you had authority over; never claiming your full inheritance but continuing to live as an orphan.

How God Sees Me

Read the following verses about how God views you:

You are the light of the world. A town built on a hill cannot be hidden (Matthew 5:14 NIV).

Then you will shine among them like stars in the sky (Philippians 2:15 NIV).

You are all children of the light and children of the day. We do not belong to the night or to the darkness (1 Thessalonians 5:5 NIV).

No, in all these things we are more than conquerors through Him who loved us (Romans 8:37 NIV).

But you are a chosen people, a royal priesthood, a holy nation, God's special possession, that you may declare the praises of Him who called you out of darkness into His wonderful light (1 Peter 2:9 NIV).

For we are God's handiwork, created in Christ Jesus to do good works, which God prepared in advance for us to do (Ephesians 2:10 NIV).

Living Forgiven

We are already forgiven for what we have done and what we will do because of the cross. Sin has no dominion over us (Romans 6:14).

So today, I want you to write your prayer to God with the understanding that you've already been forgiven and that He no longer remembers your sins. I want you to pray with joy and thanksgiving for the perfection and righteousness that you now have through Christ Jesus! Step into your new identity and passionately claim your inheritance. You are not a lowly sinner. You were once, but never again!

_____
_____
_____
_____
_____
_____
_____

Week Six - Sin and the Real Enemy

Day Four - Exchanging Lies for Truth

In week one, we read about when sin entered this world. If we trace back to the very first encounter with the enemy, we can see his divisive plan from the start. He is crafty in his desire to move us away from intimacy with God towards doubt and lies.

The First Lie

Let's look back and read Genesis 3:1-13 again.

This passage not only changes the course of history because sin entered the world but clearly shows us how easy it is to be deceived by the lies of the enemy. **In our moments of weakness, the voice of the enemy entices us to compromise what we know is truth for what the enemy feeds us through lies.**

What lie did the enemy tell Eve in the garden?

_____

_____

What was the result of her choice to believe the lie of the serpent instead of the voice of God?

_____

_____

Satan is referred to as the enemy and the father of lies. God works and moves as the voice of truth and the divisive plan of the enemy is to tear down those truths. **Sin drives us to make choices that oppose the perfect will of God in our lives.**

In John chapter 8, Jesus is talking with the religious leaders about what it means to be true children of God. Read John 8:31-47 in your Bible.

Jesus said "If you hold to my teaching, you are really my disciples. Then you will know the truth and the truth will set you free" (John 8:31 NIV).

Later in that same passage, Jesus goes on to speak to the true devastation that often misguides us.

> *Jesus said to them, "If God were your Father, you would love Me, for I have come here from God. I have not come on my own; God sent Me. Why is my language not clear to you? Because you are unable to hear what I say. You belong to your father, the devil, and you want to carry out your father's desires. He was a murderer from the beginning, not holding to the truth, for there is no truth in him. When he lies, he speaks his native language, for he is a liar and the father of lies (John 8:42-44 NIV).*

In this passage, Jesus is simply saying the enemy is a liar, and when we speak things that aren't true, we are not in line with our heavenly Father. Instead, we are choosing to come under the influence of the father of lies.

Replacing Lies with Truth

Do you often catch yourself speaking untruth that can sound and even feel like truth? The lie from the enemy that Eve believed was in contradiction to the truth God himself spoke directly to them in the garden. **Anything that stands against the nature of God or the truth in the Word is a lie from the enemy meant to bring division between us and God.**

What are the things that you believe about yourself that don't line up with the nature of God or the truth from His Word?

_____
_____
_____
_____

Events in your life can shape your beliefs about yourself, God, relationships and people. As a believer, we get to choose to identify those lies, reject them, remove them from our thinking and replace them with truth.

In our book The Original Sanctuary we introduce the concept that every ingrained behavior we may struggle with can be directly linked to a thought origin. Thoughts

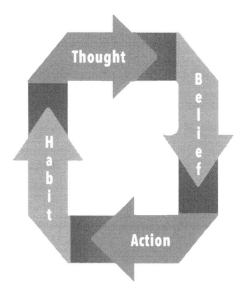

become the truth we believe about ourselves, others or a situation. Our beliefs direct our actions and repeated actions become our ingrained behavior or habits.

On the previous page we've identified a few lies, and together we will practice what to do with those lies, so that we can overcome and overthrow the father of lies.

Today I want you to ask the Father of Truth to help you identify any and all lies that you believe about yourself, about Him, about relationships and about people in your life. Remember, the father of lies likes to make them sound like truth and justifiable. If they do not line up with the nature or character of God and the truth in the Word, they're lies. Before you start, take a minute and pray, be honest, transparent, and vulnerable. This is between you and Your Father, and He will meet you right where you are.

	Lies I believe about...	Truth to declare about...
Myself		
God		
Relationships		
Others		

After you've written down the lies, I'm asking you to surrender them to Jesus, lay them down, relinquish your rights to them. Replace them with the truth from your loving Father.

Because the father of lies is a clever creature, he is constantly playing on our weaknesses and strategically attacking our strengths. Satan's number one goal is to use his lies to obstruct God's will and God's plan for our lives and the Kingdom.

The Thief is Waiting

We've identified the enemy as the father of lies. Another name for the enemy is the thief.

Grab your Bible and read John 10:1-18.

How does the thief or robber enter the sheep pen?_____

How does the shepherd enter?_____

What does the thief come to do?

_____, _____ and _____.

A thief is a person who steals another person's property, especially by stealth. The thief in our lives can be the enemy or another person under the influence of the enemy with the same motives and desires to wreak havoc in the life of a believer.

Thieves and robbers are a real threat against the will of God and the identity of a believer. Their cunning and crafty deception deprives us of abundant life we were designed for.

To **steal** by definition is to take (another person's property) without permission and without intending to return it; to take away something that isn't yours to have.

The most fitting definition of **kill** is put an end to or cause the failure or defeat of (something). The thief wants to put an end to our identity as a son or daughter of God or in this passage, as a sheep under the careful watch of the shepherd.

To **destroy** means to ruin (someone) emotionally or spiritually or defeat (someone) utterly. The plot of the thief is to mess us up spiritually and emotionally, so that all we feel is hopeless defeat.

The thief came to kill Jesus, steal the image of God in us and destroy the works of the Holy Spirit through us.

What has the thief tried to steal in your life?

_____

_____

What has the thief tried to kill in your life?

_____

_____

What has the thief tried to destroy in your life?

_____

_____

The end of John 10:10 holds the sweetest words from Jesus and the most incredible promise.

What did Jesus come to do?_____

In your own words, how would you describe a full life through Jesus?

_____
_____
_____
_____
_____
_____
_____
_____
_____

Truth Declaration

Every day we have a choice to declare the truth from God's Word over our lives. We can never get enough of the Word and applying it to our lives.

As we conclude today fill in this prayer:

Lord, You have come that I would have life, a full life. The thief has robbed me of the full life by stealing my _____,
killing my _____ and destroying my _____.
But today, I choose to take back my _____. I ask you to
resurrect my _____ and restore my _____.

Read this prayer out loud over yourself and grab hold of His promises for you!

Fear is the enemy's prophetic lie over your life. Faith is God's prophetic truth ordained for your life! Which will you choose to believe today?

Week Six - Sin and the Real Enemy

Day Five - Exchanging Our Wrong Believing for Grace

Throughout our years of ministry, we have all come to understand as a team that wrong believing produces wrong behavior. Unfortunately, there are well intended believers that are cheapening the word 'grace' and the finished work of Jesus Christ on the cross. If you believe in something that is not true, it doesn't matter how many times you practice it; you will not get good results. There's no point in addressing bad behavior; we want to pull the root and address wrong believing.

For years I believed that I had to do something to earn God's forgiveness. My heart was pure in its desire, but I was trapped by a wrong belief system. I confessed all my sins daily and sometimes minute-by-minute because I wanted to be in good standing with the Father. I kept a scorecard when I was doing really good and even harsher scorecard when I missed the mark. I was trying to earn my value with God. I earnestly asked Him to make me pleasing in His sight and help me become righteous. If we continue down that path, it robs us of our rightful place as sons and daughters and the security of being loved unconditionally. Let's look at this passage below as it relates to sin.

Living Forgiven

> When you were dead in your sins and in the uncircumcision of your flesh, God made you alive with Christ. He forgave us all our sins (Colossians 2:13 NIV).

How much of your sin did He forgive?_____

That is right, ALL. This is why they call the message of Jesus Christ GOOD NEWS! God didn't withhold any of His forgiveness. He gave it all! Past, present and future sins were forgiven the moment you asked Jesus into your heart. **We don't confess our sins for forgiveness; we confess because we are forgiven.** When we have the total assurance of forgiveness, we enter His throne room of grace boldly and confidently as the scripture says:

> So now we come freely and boldly to where love is enthroned, to receive mercy's kiss and discover the grace we urgently need to strengthen us in our time of weakness (Hebrews 4:16 TPT).

Did you notice that the scripture says to "strengthen us?" Most of the time we believe that He is condemning us. **When we partner with the Holy Spirit, He will strengthen us in the righteousness of Christ.**

> So now the case is closed. There remains no accusing voice of condemnation against those who are joined in life-union with Jesus, the Anointed One. For the "law" of the Spirit of life flowing through the anointing of Jesus has liberated us from the "law" of sin and death. For God achieved what the law was unable to accomplish, because the law was limited by the weakness of human nature. Yet God sent us His Son in human form to identify with human weakness. Clothed with humanity, God's Son gave his body to be the sin-offering so that God could once and for all condemn the guilt and power of sin. So now every righteous requirement of the law can be fulfilled through the Anointed One living His life in us. And we are free to live, not according to our flesh, but by the dynamic power of the Holy Spirit (Romans 8:1-5 TPT).

> He Himself bore our sins in His body on the tree, that we might die to sin and live to righteousness. By His wounds you have been healed (1 Peter 2:24 ESV).

We have been called to receive the righteousness of Jesus' work on the cross. God can't condemn you because you no longer live, but rather Christ lives in you. Sin can't define you because of the power of grace and God's love. **You are no longer judged by your works or sin but rather judged through the perfect work of Jesus.**

Receiving Love and Forgiveness

Please do not misunderstand me. I believe we have been called to be transparent, real, raw and unreligious when we do miss the mark. We have not been called to sweep sin under the rug and hide in the dark alone. I call those people posers.

However, as sons and daughters, we can be confident that God is not surprised by our sin. He simply wants us to start focusing on His love instead of trying to work for our righteousness.

He wants us to shift our focus from our mess-ups to His goodness. Just the other day I was running errands before work and realized I forgot my computer at the house. I was frustrated and disappointed in myself as I was backtracking to the house to get my computer. About halfway home, the Holy Spirit shifted my focus from my mess-up to His love that was at work in my life. I began to thank Him for reminding me that I didn't have my computer when I was ten minutes away from my house instead of fifty minutes away from my house. I also recognized how quick I am to get frustrated and miss Him at work in me. Oh, how often we just need a little adjustment on our perspective to be able to see Him in the midst of it all.

As we conclude this week, journal your thoughts and continue to shift your focus from your sin to His grace and love. **Gratitude is the greatest expression of faith and the best way to overcome the evil one, grow in grace and truth and stand in victory daily.** In your prayer journal, start writing down a few things you are grateful for every single day.

Find Him in the hard stuff, the mess ups, the victories and the little blessings that come throughout your day.

_____
_____
_____
_____
_____
_____
_____
_____
_____
_____
_____
_____
_____
_____
_____
_____
_____
_____

Week Six - Sin and the Real Enemy

Day Six - Resting Our Physical Bodies

We've talked about how we are made up of three parts: body, soul and spirit. When our body and soul are at rest, then our spirit can connect with and be led by His Spirit.

Body rest is about our physical bodies and it is one of the easiest and hardest things for us. We misinterpret rest as sleeping in on a Saturday or taking a nap. True rest for our bodies can be sitting still in a recliner for 10 minutes at the end of a work day, jumping in the pool for a quick swim after mowing the yard, or fixing a cup of tea or coffee and sitting down to enjoy a good book in the middle of the day. I know that sounds crazy, but our bodies are moving at the same pace as our minds, and when we get fatigued, everything else is impacted or affected.

Today we get to be mindful of our physical body. We can take time to physically rest throughout the day. Rest can look like sitting down with your toddler curled up in your lap reading a book. Rest can be a ride on the four-wheeler at the deer lease. Rest can look like 20 minutes on the hammock outside. Rest can look like sitting in your Lazy Boy chair but not being lazy. Rest can look like sitting at your desk and not working, just taking a minute to breathe and rest your mind.

It's important for us to find opportunities to allow our physical bodies to rest. When I was training for a half marathon, putting in the hours of running and training were important; but just as important as the hours and miles logged on the trails were the days of rest. It was important for my body to rebuild the muscles that had been broken down in my training time.

We have such a hard time seeing this applied in our daily lives.

If you're going to work at anything, work at rest. It's the hardest thing for us to do but one of our greatest needs. Today let's make it a point to rest physically. Ceasing activity even just for a few minutes can allow you to regain focus, peace and the ability to be led by the Holy Spirit, who gives you the strength and energy to tackle the next activity or project.

What are a few ways that you can be proactive about rest today?

- _____
- _____
- _____
- _____
- _____
- _____
- _____
- _____
- _____
- _____

Meditate on this passage:

> "Come to Me, all you who are weary and burdend, and I will give you rest. Take My yoke upon you and learn from Me, for I am gentle and humble in heart, and you will find rest for your souls. For My yoke is easy and My burden is light." (Matthew 11:28-30).

Our Identity

As I learn to live out my God-given identity and believe what He says is true about me, faith becomes my strength and trust becomes my anchor.

Week Seven - Our Identity

Day One - We are Sons and Daughters of God

"When God selected you, it doesn't matter who else has rejected or neglected you. God's favor outweighs them all!" -elevateHim

The task of writing and adequately describing our identity in Christ makes me feel like a little boy who has been given the job of filling up the Grand Canyon with dirt by lunch time with a bucket and small shovel. It is a big task, but we'll start with one shovel at a time.

If you could look inside the heart of the Father, you will see at the very center that it is full of love for people. Yes, it's full of love, peace, patience, power and lots of other things, but His heart bleeds people. We were created in His image as we discussed in week one. **God is not just the God of love, but in fact, He is the God that loves people!**

When you realize that God loves people, then and only then, can you begin to see that His heart is firmly and securely rooted in His precious children. Some people see God as a dictator. Whether or not that belief paints Him as a benevolent dictator or a ruthless one depends on the individual's experience, knowledge and personal encounter with God. God is not a dictator, but rather a loving Father. This is demonstrated through His love expressed towards His son, Jesus, and Jesus's expression of love towards us.

God Speaks our Identity as Sons and Daughters

We see God's fatherly interaction with Jesus at the beginning of His ministry. As Jesus is baptized in the Jordan River, the heavens part, and a dove descends. The Father's voice shatters the silence, and God declares that Jesus is *"My Son, whom I love; with Him I am well pleased"* (Matthew 3:17; Mark 1:11; Luke 3:22). We begin to discover that our identity is rooted as a son or daughter of God. In fact, scripture describes us as *"sons and daughters"* of *"the Lord Almighty"* (2 Corinthians 6:18).

Scripture also depicts God as a loving, welcoming and a gracious Father who abounds in love for all who accept His son, Jesus, into their hearts.

Jesus, in turn, begins to pour out the same expression of love when his disciples ask him how to pray.

> *"This, then, is how you should pray: 'Our Father in heaven, hallowed be your name, your kingdom come, your will be done, on earth as it is in heaven. Give us today our daily bread. And forgive us our debts, as we also have forgiven our debtors. And lead us not into temptation but deliver us from the evil one'"* (Matthew 6:9-13 NIV).

Jesus rapidly begins to equip His disciples with the truth about their royal identity and God's love as our Heavenly Father. **Your identity is assigned value by the One who values you.** Jesus makes it obvious. We are valued and loved by our Father, who not only watches from heaven but sent His son to walk with us on this journey. Human nature was infected at the beginning with a deadly disease (sin) that caused us to feel alone and many times orphaned, abandoned by love.

I want to continue to remind you that the Father gave the Son, and the Son gave the Holy Spirit to us. The Spirit of God leads us because we are His children. We bear the God-given right to be called sons and daughters of God. When we receive this, it becomes the foundation of our identity.

> *For as many as are led by the Spirit of God, these are sons of God. For you did not receive the spirit of bondage again to fear, but you received the Spirit of adoption by whom we cry out, "Abba, Father." The Spirit Himself bears witness with our spirit that we are children of God* (Romans 8:14-16 NKJV).

In response to this passage, have you embraced your identity as a son/daughter of God? How does this affect your daily living and interactions with others? Journal below:

_____
_____
_____

This week our verse to commit to memory is Galatians 4:7.

> *So you are no longer a slave, but God's child, and since you are His child; God has made you also an heir* (Galations 4:7 NIV).

Week Seven - Our Identity

Day Two - We are a New Creation

When we have confessed Jesus as Lord of our lives, we are in Christ. This statement speaks to our new identity as a son or daughter and is the new directive for how we live our lives and live our faith in the One who saved us.

> *Therefore, if anyone is in Christ, the new creation has come: The old has gone, the new is here* (2 Corinthians 5:17 NIV).

The word "therefore" refers us back to verses 14-16 where Paul tells us that all believers have died with Christ and no longer live for themselves.

Let Go of the Old

As a runner, there's one thing that can make or break you...your shoes. Running shoes are designed to be worn for hundreds of miles, but how you use or abuse them and take care of them determines how long they last. When a runner's feet start to hurt, there's usually a simple solution...new shoes. Now it's possible, if I get them dirty, I can clean them up a little, but buying new running shoes is the only way to solve the dilemma of pain from worn out shoes.

This scripture speaks clearly to Christians that the old you has gone, and the new you is here to stay. We get to choose to believe this on a daily basis. Whether or not we believe this truth is reflected in our everyday choices, words and actions.

As a believer, I am faced daily with the temptation to revert back to my old ways or to boldly walk in full belief in the new direction God has called me to go.

It's easy to buy new running shoes when my feet start to hurt but hard to throw the old ones away. I try and use them for everyday shoes or work shoes or whatever else I can think of to use them for. The problem: at the end of the day my feet hurt, and I'm reminded why I bought new shoes. I tell you this story because it perfectly parallels to life in Christ. For whatever reason, we cling to old habits or relationships from our "old life" afraid we might be getting rid of something we want to hold onto.

Is there anything from your "old life" before Christ that is hard for you to let go of?

_____

_____

Embrace the New

This scripture in 2 Corinthians 5:17 tells us clearly the old has gone and the new has come. The new has replaced the old, and there's no space for it anymore. In the same way, living a life of knowing and loving God because of His great love for us replaces our rights to the lies we've been believing. We can no longer live as an orphan instead of a son or daughter of God.

We must choose daily what we allow to be our defining truth: old lies or new truth. TIME TO THROW AWAY THE OLD SHOES.

What are some old lies that try and come back at you?

_____

_____

What are the new truths God wants you to embrace to replace the old lies?

_____

_____

Continue moment by moment, day-by-day, to allow the new you to remain in place of the old you. As the old tries to creep back in, get still and get in the Word, so that you are reminded of the truth. Invite others you can trust into this journey with you. The familiar pain that comes with the old can either be chronic or remind us that we have a new truth to live by.

I can walk around in shoes that cause my feet to hurt or throw them away and enjoy my new shoes pain-free. Are you ready to put on your new shoes? It's your decision. The Bible says we should shod ourselves with the readiness that comes from the gospel of peace (Ephesians 6:15).

Let's put on the new shoes so that we can run the race GOD HAS CALLED US TO. Enjoy the race! Live like the new creation He says we are!

Week Seven - Our Identity

Day Three - We are His

Our identity can be firmly rooted in the truth of the Word. God's Word clearly tells us who we are in great detail. It also tells us whose we are.

> *For you are a people holy to the Lord your God. The Lord your God has chosen you out of all the peoples on the face of the earth to be his people, his treasured possession. The Lord did not set his affection on you and choose you because you were more numerous than other peoples, for you were the fewest of all peoples. But it was because the Lord loved you and kept the oath he swore to your ancestors that He brought you out with a mighty hand and redeemed you from the land of slavery, from the power of Pharaoh king of Egypt. Know therefore that the Lord your God is God; he is the faithful God, keeping His covenant of love to a thousand generations of those who love Him and keep His commandments (Deuteronomy 7:6-9 NIV).*

As you read that scripture what stands out to you?

_____

_____

_____

_____

Read back through the scripture above and circle every word that describes who you are to Him.

We are His Chosen People

You are His people. Walking in relationships with others, we tend to find a group that we belong to. Once we build relationships and invest some time, we say something like "these are my people." The thing is, God chose us to be "His people" long before we started having our people.

He chose us, and we are holy to Him. Let that soak in for a minute. What does it mean to be holy to the Lord? (1 Peter 1:15)

_____

_____

_____

We are His Treasured Possession

Think about your most treasured possession. For most of us, when we hear that, we think of an object. Truth be told, people are not and cannot be our possessions because they are already someone else's. Our favorite possession could be a car or a piece of jewelry, an heirloom or family photos. Whatever it is, if we value it, we take care of it. A car we take for regular oil changes, maintenance and car washes. Jewelry we wear proudly, store safely, and clean when it needs cleaning. You get the point. If we treasure it, we protect it, take care of it and show it off proudly.

As a treasured possession of a loving Father, I can trust that He is caring intently for me, protecting me, watching me and celebrating me.

What is something you treasure and how do you care for it?

_____

_____

_____

We are Loved by Him

The passage goes on to say; He chose us because He loves us. Because He loves us, He brought us out of the land of slavery. I don't know what your Egypt was, but for the Israelites, it was horrific. There was abuse. They were mistreated, belittled, and told they were worthless. Worse than being treated as if they were worthless was the reality that many of them believed they deserved it. They couldn't even imagine a life outside of the slavery they had known for so long.

For many of us, we live like the slaves stuck in Egypt instead of the chosen and treasured possession we are. Our slavery can look like addiction, depression, fear, insecurity, or unbelief. **If we aren't willing to take God at His Word and wear our true identity as a badge of honor, we continue to live fruitless and pain-filled lives.**

Is there anything you feel like you are still enslaved to instead of living loved? Share that with God in a prayer. He already knows, but freedom comes as we are honest with ourselves and Him. Ask Him to show you His love in a real way right now.

_____

_____

His Love Motivates Us

Deuteronomy 7:6-9 goes on to say, He is a faithful God, keeping His covenant of love to those who love Him and keep His commandments. All of this is motivated by love. His love for us motivates us to love Him and obey Him. No matter how hard we try to love Him or obey Him, we can't earn His love. You can't earn something that's already yours. In the same way, if we mess up or disobey, His love doesn't change. You can't lose something that is yours forever regardless of your actions. Our position as His chosen people and treasured possession is ours forever. We just get to learn to live like we believe the truth.

Write a prayer in response to His truth and declarations in this passage. Tell Him in your own words who you are to Him as stated in Deuteronomy 7:6-9.

_____

_____

_____

_____

_____

_____

_____

_____

_____

_____

_____

_____

_____

_____

_____

_____

Fear is the enemy's scare tactic of "what if" over your life. FAITH is God's declaration over your life of "what will be!" Who do you want to partner with?

Week Seven - Our Identity

Day Four - We Have a Purpose

"The devil's greatest trick is to convince you that you're not who God says you are." -elevateHim Team

As a believer, we are all called to the exact same thing, to love the Lord with everything in us and share that love with the world. How we accomplish that is personal and individual. We are all commanded to love God and love people, but we are uniquely wired to create, and as we walk in our identity, we can each fulfill our specific purpose.

> *For it is by grace you have been saved, through faith—and this is not from yourselves, it is the gift of God— not by works, so that no one can boast. For we are God's handiwork, created in Christ Jesus to do good works, which God prepared in advance for us to do (Ephesians 2:8-10 NIV).*

God prepared us from the beginning of time to do good works. We are only able to do these good works because of our love relationship with Him. As we pursue Him, He gives us everything we need to pour out His love on the world.

God has a plan for our lives. I think it's easy for all of us to agree on that. God has predestined us to be his sons and daughters. We unpacked that on day 1.

Take a minute and read through this passage in Ephesians chapter 1.

> *Praise be to the God and Father of our Lord Jesus Christ, who has blessed us in the heavenly realms with every spiritual blessing in Christ. For He chose us in Him before the creation of the world to be holy and blameless in his sight. In love He predestined us for adoption to sonship through Jesus Christ, in accordance with his pleasure and*

will—to the praise of His glorious grace, which He has freely given us in the One He loves. In Him we have redemption through His blood, the forgiveness of sins, in accordance with the riches of God's grace that He lavished on us. With all wisdom and understanding, He made known to us the mystery of His will according to His good pleasure, which He purposed in Christ, to be put into effect when the times reach their fulfillment—to bring unity to all things in heaven and on earth under Christ. In Him we were also chosen, having been predestined according to the plan of Him who works out everything in conformity with the purpose of His will, in order that we, who were the first to put our hope in Christ, might be for the praise of His glory. And you also were included in Christ when you heard the message of truth, the gospel of your salvation. When you believed, you were marked in Him with a seal, the promised Holy Spirit, who is a deposit guaranteeing our inheritance until the redemption of those who are God's possession—to the praise of his glory (Ephesians 1:3-12 NIV).

Go through the passage and circle everything he has done for us or calls us. In the box put a check-mark next to the ones that are easy for you to believe and an "X" next to the ones that are harder.

> My name is _____
> God blessed ME
> God chose ME
> God calls ME blameless
> God predestined ME
> God has made His will known to ME
> God works everything for MY purpose
> God made ME for His glory
> God marked ME with a seal
> God has freely bgiven ME His grace
> I have redemption through His blood
> God offers ME forgiveness of sins
> God gave ME Holy Spirit
> God gave ME an inheritance

WOW! That's a lot packed into a small passage of scripture, and the Bible is full of plenty more like this. The greatest challenge is for us to believe that all of this is true about us.

Our Purpose

We read these scriptures and must choose to cling to them as truth. **We were designed from the beginning of time to be loved by Him, to know Him personally, to love Him, and to share Him with others.** Our purpose can be summed up in the great commandment:

Teacher, which is the greatest commandment in the Law? Jesus replied: "'Love the Lord your God with all your heart and with all your soul and with all your mind.' This is the first and greatest commandment. And the second is like it: Love your neighbor as yourself. All the Law and the Prophets hang on these two commandments." (Matthew 22:36-40 NIV).

Here, the Pharisees are actually trying to trick Jesus. He turns it back towards them and makes a bold statement. **Jesus is greater than the law and the prophets.** As co-heirs with Christ we are only capable of fulfilling this commandment through the grace and truth of Jesus Christ.

It's impossible to do this in our own strength apart from the love of God for us. We must allow the love and Spirit of God to move in and through us for all to receive His love. We get to be conduits of His love to others.

Our Calling

How we fulfill this great commandment is as diverse and unique as the stars in the universe. We get caught up in semantics and ponder or wonder what our calling in life might be. Your calling is the way God designed you to fulfill your God-given purpose. For some it is to write. Others sing, build, draw, or play instruments. It can also be the way you pray, organize or clean, serve others, encourage through spoken or written words, bake meals or volunteer at the nursing home.

Our calling is the thing for which we were created. As a believer in Jesus Christ, we all have the same purpose.

Complete these statements in your own words:

My purpose is to_____
_____
_____
_____
_____
_____
_____
_____
_____

My calling that I was uniquely created and wired for is_____

_____

_____

_____

_____

_____

_____

Now write a prayer surrendering all of this to Him. Ask Him to open the doors for you to fulfill your calling as you learn to walk unashamed in your purpose.

Week Seven - Our Identity

Day Five - We Live by Faith

Faith is the expression of our trust in the Lord above any circumstance we experience.

Without faith it is impossible to please God (Hebrews 11:6b NIV).

Maybe you have heard this scripture before, it is nestled in what I like to call the "Faith Hall-of-Fame" chapter. Take a minute and read Hebrews chapter 11 in your Bible and underline every time the word <u>faith</u> is used.

I Have Been Crucified with Christ

I have been crucified with Christ and I no longer live, but Christ lives in me. The life I now live in the body, I live by faith in the Son of God, who loved me and gave himself for me. I do not set aside the grace of God, for if righteousness could be gained through the law, Christ died for nothing (Galatians 2:20-21 NIV).

When we hear the word "crucified" we immediately go to the images of the cross we have in our heads based on the movies we've seen. *The Passion of the Christ* is hard to watch. To see the torture Jesus endured leading up to his death, rocks us to our core. We can unintentionally make light of the true reality of what it means to be crucified with Christ.

If I am crucified with Christ, I too will experience the pain from the death of one thing for the life of another. Being crucified with Christ means that I am putting to death my flesh to fully surrender to the will of God. Every selfish desire and ambition can be submitted to the perfect will of God. Our greatest obstacles to living by faith can be the selfish desire to please myself, partnering with the lies of the enemy and trying to achieve security through works.

As I learn to live out my God-given identity and believe what He says is true about me, faith becomes my strength and trust becomes my anchor.

Before Christ, I was sinful and selfish. The grace afforded to me through the cross says something completely different. The key to living like I believe the truth and trust what He says about me is found through faith in the only One who has the authority to speak my identity.

My Flesh Does Not Win

We aren't defined by who we think we are or are not, but by who He says we are. We cannot overcome our sinful nature on our own. We try to strong arm our tendencies toward sin and fall short or end up exhausted every time. You want to know why? Because we weren't called to a life of sin management, perfection or performance. **We were called to a life of living out our God-given identity and embracing the grace, love and truth of God given to us through Jesus and the Holy Spirit.**

We need to lean into and call on the Holy Spirit to make this happen. **Surrendering our will to God's will is essential to living free and walking in our identity as sons and daughters, chosen and dearly loved.** When we surrender our flesh to be crucified with Christ, we relinquish our rights and control to the power and will of the Holy Spirit.

I like to eat. A wise woman in my life once said, "I don't live to eat, I eat to live," and she truly lives that way. She doesn't get excited about food at all. I on the other hand, live to eat. I wake up thinking about my first, second and third meal of the day. There have been a few times that the Lord has called me to an extended fast because my desire for food far outweighed my desire for Him. In those times, I had the opportunity to learn, again, what it means to be crucified with Christ.

Throughout my fast I had to deny (crucify) my flesh because I desired more of Him in place of me. It was painful and hard. Social environments are full of opportunities to compromise or walk in our flesh. I was committed to obedience; motivated by my love for Him and His love for me. Because of this, I was able to walk through that season, and there was growth through the sacrifice. He is alive in me, and it was His strength fueling my faith every meal of everyday.

I could have dominated this fast because I'm regimented and committed, desiring to do it perfectly. I could have denied myself to prove something to myself or others, but the alternative was to learn to live in the place of grace where He gives me everything I need, including the strength to deny my flesh, take up my cross and follow Him.

Grace Wins Every Time

In order to live a life that is fully His, I get to move out of the driver's seat and let Him lead. Our tendency will always be to jump back in the driver's seat and take control, but by the grace given to us through Jesus, we can live surrendered and dependent on Christ who lives in us. The key we cannot miss that is paramount to us walking in our God-given identity is…(drum-roll please!!!!!!!) GRACE!

Everything, and I mean everything, points back to grace. As we wrap up this week together, let's write our own personal truth declarations. There are no rules or right or wrong way, but let's start with re-stating what's already been mentioned this week. It is by the grace of God that we can claim and declare the truth of who we are without shame or doubt. Together we are walking in our most incredible identity!

I AM _____

I AM _____

I AM _____

I AM _____

I AM _____

I AM _____

I AM _____

I AM _____

I AM _____

I AM _____

I AM _____

I AM _____

Week Seven - Our Identity

Day Six - Resting in Joy

The joy of the Lord is our strength (Nehemiah 8:10 NIV). In every hard situation and painful place, His joy is our strength. No matter what we are facing today, we are encouraged to face it with JOY. Joy is easy to talk about, but it seems hard to remain in it.

What brings delight to you? (Make a list of everything that brings you JOY).

- _____   - _____

- _____   - _____

- _____   - _____

When your joy is under attack, I can guarantee your faith is growing. When we can find joy in the hard stuff, it equals growth in our spiritual life. **Acknowledgment of God's presence, protection and provision keeps us grounded in gratitude and keeps us in a place of joy.**

Romans 15:13 (NIV) makes this declaration *"May the God of hope fill you with all joy and peace as you trust in Him that you may overflow with hope by the power of the Holy Spirit."*

One way we can remain in a place of joy is through gratitude and perspective. The right perspective gives us the ability to see the right things the right way. If truth is your perspective concerning the subject of joy, then a vehicle to joy is gratitude.

We can give thanks with a grateful heart every day in every situation. Many may ask how I would deal with abuse, illness, or tragedy. Bad things happen, but the joy of the Lord remains. We choose to see things that happen through the eyes of the

One who knows all things and is in all things. He is working all things for the good of those who love Him and are called according to His purpose (Romans 8:28).

As we learn to rest in joy, we must redirect our physical and emotional eyes from the painful places to the joy of the Lord through supernatural gratitude.

Bottom line, we all have hard things that happen to us or those we love. They can be the excuses for why we choose not to live in joy, but as we said in the beginning, it comes down to perspective. The perspective of truth that all things work together for our good because He loves us will redirect our hearts and minds to the One who does the work for us.

No matter what life throws at us or what hard situation we end up in, we choose to count it joy. Grab hold of joy and walk in grace, truth, and trust.

Now in light of what we've talked about, knowing every good and hard thing can and will be used by Him, make a list of all the things you will count as joy today. You can rest in this: He loves you; He sees you; He knows your pain; and His joy will be your strength.

- _____   - _____

- _____   - _____

- _____   - _____

- _____   - _____

- _____   - _____

- _____   - _____

How often do we get frustrated that our kids aren't grateful for what they have, what we've worked so hard to provide for them? When was the last time you thanked God for EVERY GOOD THING in your life? Did you thank God that your car starts each morning you need it to go to work? Are you grateful that you have clean water to bathe in and drink and cook with? In a nation rampant with entitlement and selfishness, we can forget to acknowledge who God is and what He provides. These are all blessings and deserve a grateful heart.

How do we find the joy that we feel like we are missing? Gratitude. **When we remain in a place of gratitude, it can be the staple-part of our diet that fuels our joy.**

Ask Holy Spirit for the right perspective to see His blessing and provision in every area of your life today. Take time today to write a prayer thanking Him for every little and big thing.

_____

_____

_____

_____

_____

_____

_____

_____

_____

_____

_____

_____

_____

_____

_____

_____

_____

_____

_____

_____

_____

_____

_____

_____

_____

_____

_____

Living in Relationships

Freedom comes when we learn to live in real, authentic relationship with others. We were created to love God and love others. Living in relationship with other believers is a crucial part of our faith walk.

Week Eight - Living in Relationships

Day One - My Relationship with God

The most important relationship in my life is my relationship with God. When I build my foundation on the truth from God's Word and His inexplicable love for me, everything else falls into place. Even when the hard stuff comes against me, my foundation is immovable when it's firmly rooted in grace, love and truth.

Every great block tower requires one thing, a strong foundation. You can build on a strong foundation and work your way up, but if the foundation is weak, you won't be able to get far.

Recently while playing a game of Jenga with friends, I saw this illustrated right before my eyes. If you have never played Jenga, picture this: a tower made with rectangular blocks; each layer of blocks laid on top of the previous layer, alternating direction to create a strong foundation; each piece partnered with two other pieces and each layer strong because of the three pieces laid together. As you play the game, you begin to pull out pieces from each layer finding the loose ones and re-stacking them on the top of the tower. The foundation or base of the tower weakens as you remove the pieces one at a time until the tower comes tumbling down. A shaky foundation becomes a liability for every player involved.

Our faith walk is similar. Without a strong foundation, our towers are shaky and become hazardous to our family, friends and people we do life with.

Imagine your life as a block tower, built by every choice you make on a daily basis.

What's at the foundation of your life? What have you built your tower on?

_____

_____

_____

_____

Another fun fact about building is you never build a block tower from the top down. It's impossible. The same is true in our pursuit of Jesus and living fully alive. We must build from the bottom up on a strong, secure foundation.

We've been walking together through these last seven weeks to help you lay a foundation that you can build on for the rest of your life. Together we have unpacked the basics, learned how to dig into the Word, connected to Jesus through the cross, embraced grace by faith, engaged God through prayer, practiced hearing God, found confidence in our identity, and identified sin -- its origin and our freedom from it.

This last week together we will learn to live in relationship connected to God, ourselves and others.

My relationship with God is the most important relationship in my life. How I live my life on a daily basis, the words that come out of my mouth, and the people who are impacted through me are all directly affected by my connection with and proximity to God.

God wants nothing more than for us to seek Him and know Him. *"Then you will call upon me and come and pray to me, and I will listen to you. You will seek me and find me when you search for me with all your heart. I will be found by you,"* declares the Lord (Jeremiah 29:12-14 NIV).

My relationship with God is two-sided. I speak; He speaks. I give; He gives. He sacrificed; I sacrifice. I surrender; He shows up.

He doesn't keep Himself hidden from me, but am I on the journey to find Him?

God wants me to know and understand, encounter and accept HIS LOVE FOR ME. As evidence of this understanding, I love Him through prayer, my two-way conversation with Him, how I live my life and what I do with the blessings He's given me.

- Do I know His love for me?
- Do I understand His love for me?
- Have I encountered His love for me?
- Have I accepted His love for me?

In Psalm 46:10 He asks us to be still and know that He is God. It's in our stillness, not our doing, that He wants to show us who He is. In every relationship, there's a courting period where you are trying to get to know each other and decide if you want to continue the relationship. Once you commit to continue, you ask more questions, listen more intently, dig deeper into their stories and spend more time together. You celebrate what brings them joy and weep with them when they are broken.

Keys to a healthy relationship with God:

- Commit to the relationship.
- Get to know Him.
- Ask questions.
- Celebrate who He is and what He is doing.
- Listen intently.
- Dig deeper.
- Spend time together.
- Stop striving to gain approval.

We must be willing to press into our relationship with God and pursue Him to develop a healthy, strong foundation to build our lives on. As we do, He reveals Himself in so many ways. **When we are looking for Him in the everyday moments of our lives, He shows up and shows off.**

For me, I love hearts. Heart-shaped things show up at the most random times in the most random places. I look for them now and notice them. I can be on a run at the park and see a heart-shaped leaf on the trail, and as soon as I see it, it draws me into conversation with Him. "God, I see you. I love you. I know you're here with me." My son finds heart-shaped rocks almost every time he's at the deer lease and sends me a picture or brings them home to me. God uses every single one of them as reminders of His love for me and His presence in my life. I get text messages with pictures of heart-shaped french fries or chips from random people, and in those moments, the Lord is connecting with my heart through one of His people.

Our relationship with God is fun. He loves us and wants nothing more than for us to live like we believe it. Even when it's hard, and we feel like the world around us is falling apart, He wants to show up for us and show off in our lives in the most outrageous and unexpected ways. But His showing up in outrageous and unexpected ways can seem very small and even insignificant if you let it.

My question is, are you looking for HIM? Are you pursuing a relationship with Him fueled by His love for you or fueled by rules and expectations? Take a minute and write down your responses to these questions.

_____

_____

_____

Acknowledging God's goodness and faithfulness in your life through gratitude is one of the easiest ways to build a foundation of love and trust with your Creator. Finish today by making a list of the big and little times that God has shown up on your behalf and shown His love to you in tangible ways.

I've seen God show up through:

- _____
- _____
- _____
- _____
- _____
- _____
- _____
- _____
- _____
- _____
- _____

- _____
- _____
- _____
- _____
- _____
- _____
- _____
- _____
- _____
- _____

This week our verse to memorize and meditate on is:

Ecclesiastes 4:9-10 (NIV). *Two are better than one, because they have a good return for their labor. If either of them falls down, one can help the other up. But pity anyone who falls and has no one to help them up.*

Week Eight - Living in Relationships

Day Two - My Relationship with Myself

Sometimes the greatest definer of my personal relationship with God and others is my relationship with myself. My capacity to love God and love others is reflective of my ability or inability to love myself.

You'll never see a confident person and think "Man, that's unattractive!"

I Am Who He Says I Am

When my identity is defined by who He says I am, I am able to love the person He created. The flip side is if I'm unwilling to love myself, I am despising God's creation. **It's one thing to know who He says I am. It's another thing to live like I believe it.**

Listen to this story of one person's inner dialogue about himself:

How do I even explain what it's like to be me? Could you explain all the voices, thoughts and pictures you have of others and yourself? Sometimes I feel like I have thoughts coming from every direction, and their travel companions (called emotions) make the equation of life more complicated. In the middle of all these thoughts and emotions that make me very tender, there seems to be this battle-ready warrior that is afraid of nothing and ready to launch up the side of a mountain to rescue the sons and daughters of God. It's all very overwhelming and honestly has me asking at times if a man is supposed to feel such a wide range of emotions. People might say I was a little crazy or broken. Nevertheless, it is all of the uniqueness that makes me, me!

Want more honesty and vulnerability? How do I learn to accept myself and just embrace this collage of giftings and weaknesses? The answer has been woven together in the pages of this book. God's greatest desire is for me (and you) to see ourselves the way He sees us. We are not messed up, screwed up, washed up or unlovable. He loves all of us, even the parts that make us feel weak and vulnerable in relationships with others.

Here is the truth we all need to receive, believe and obey every day: when we allow the love of God to become personal and real for us in the middle of our beautiful collage of thoughts, feelings and emotions, then and only then, are we able to offer that same love to others.

I see so many people helping other people but abandoning themselves completely. It sounds really spiritual and honorable, but it's not at all. Abandonment is abandonment. Stop abandoning yourself. It's not spiritual, and it sure isn't love! The Holy Spirit loves you so much that He lives inside of you. He desires you to receive comfort for yourself first before you try to give it away. You can't give away what you haven't received, and if you do, then in my opinion, you are just speaking words, but they have no real power.

So for me, I end with this: "God thank you that I am fearfully and wonderfully made. I am perfect in your sight through the work of Jesus Christ. You not only love me but really like me. I choose to love myself the way You love me. I celebrate who I am today with the same joy and love You do when You celebrate me!"

Are you ready to love yourself the way He loves you? If so, write it out as your prayer to Him today.

_____
_____
_____
_____
_____
_____
_____

I am Responsible for Me

We get to self-manage our thoughts and how we allow them to impact our lives. As a believer, I have a responsibility to monitor my inner conversations. Are they uplifting or condemning? The dialogue I allow to bounce around inside my head can make or break me. **I can live enslaved to everything I'm not or live empowered because of everything He says I am.**

We demolish arguments and every pretension that sets itself up against the knowledge of God, and we take captive every thought to make it obedient to Christ (2 Corinthians 10:5 NIV).

What are the thoughts ping-ponging around in your head right now? List them below:

- _____
- _____
- _____

- _____
- _____
- _____

In all honesty, my list could look something like this:

- I can't do this. I don't have what it takes.
- Why would I think my kids would be making good choices? I made a ton of wrong ones!
- I'm a bad dad/mom.
- I have no friends. No one cares about me.
- My boss doesn't like me.
- I'm not tall/fit/skinny/strong enough.
- I need to work harder to prove something.

To counteract all those negative thoughts fighting for my heart, mind and attention, I can instead mediate on His love. Then the conversation changes and so will my belief system!

Instead of focusing on all the negative thoughts, let's take back control and make a list of truths we can meditate on today in place of the negative thoughts trying to hijack our minds and hearts. Write your truths below AND on a note-card or post-it note to carry with you today as a reminder.

- Truth #1: _I can do all things through Christ who strengthens me._ Phillipians 4:13_____
- Truth #2: _____
- Truth #3: _____
- Truth #4: _____
- Truth #5: _____

Week Eight - Living in Relationships

Day Three - My Relationship with Others

Freedom comes when we learn to live in real, authentic relationship with others. We were created to love God and love others. Living in relationship with other believers is a crucial part of our faith walk.

When we embrace the truth of God, He releases our unique purpose of being loved and giving love.

We also understand that the majority of rejection, hurt, and pain has happened within the context of relationships. What we do with our brokenness can either make us or break us.

Today we will take the time to understand God's design for relationship with others, how we relate to them, and the blessings that come from God through relationships.

Before we dive in, I want you to answer these questions with the first thought that comes to mind.

What words would you use to describe a true friend?

_____

_____

What is your greatest need in friendship/community?

_____

_____

What makes you feel loved/valued?

_____

_____

How good are you at communicating your needs in the context of friendship?

_____

_____

A few things the Word says about friendship:

> *A friend loves at all times, and a brother is born for adversity* (Prov. 17:17 NIV).

> *A gossip betrays a confidence, but a trustworthy man keeps a secret* (Proverbs 11:13 NIV).

> *A trustworthy envoy brings healing* (Proverbs 13:17b NIV).

> *A man of many companions may come to ruin but there is a friend who sticks closer than a brother* (Proverbs 18:24 NIV).

> *Wounds from a friend can be trusted* (Proverbs 27:6a NIV).

> *Perfume and incense bring joy to the heart, and the pleasantness of one's friend springs from his earnest counsel* (Proverbs 27:9 NIV).

> *As iron sharpens iron so one man sharpens another* (Proverbs 27:17 NIV).

Proverbs has a lot to say about relationships. We've talked about being sons and daughters of God, but we are also brothers and sisters to every other Christ-follower. We must take the time to love and be loved by others. Here are a few things I learned while studying what I like to call the "Proverbs Principles of Friendship."

- Good friends are dependable.
- Good friends are honest.
- Good friends are teachable.
- Good friends are trustworthy.
- Good friends speak the truth in love.

Friendship serves two primary purposes: encouragement and accountability. Does this friend help me be a better me? Challenge me to grow? Speak to and call out my strengths? Hold my feet to the fire if I'm missing it with my kids, spouse or even as a friend?

Someone once called me out for not returning their text messages. It stung for a minute but challenged me to see another's perspective and point of view. I needed to communicate even if I didn't have time to engage in that moment, so they didn't feel ignored. I never want to give the enemy fuel to add to the fire that he's trying to nurse in someone else's life.

Relationships require commitment, sacrifice, and a willingness to walk through the good stuff and the hard stuff together. Real relationships are authentic and vulnerable, transparent and real. We talk in depth about this in our book *All-In*. (Shameless plug… if you haven't read it, we highly recommend it!)

Here are a few things we can work on as we develop relationships with those around us.

Remember, God gives us five Kingdom currencies to invest in others: time, talent, treasures, word and touch. How are you investing those in relationships today?

The art of showing up -- your presence is powerful. Sometimes just showing up when you're invited or coming to a friend's kid's sporting event speaks loudly to their value in your life.

The act of serving selflessly -- do that thing you don't love doing for the sake of someone else. Help those friends move or sign up for the meal train and cook the meal. Be willing to serve others now just as you would if Jesus were staying the weekend at your house.

The power of personal connection -- Your words matter. Texts, phone calls, lunch meet-ups, baseball games, girls or guys nights are all great ways to connect. We often think we don't have time to do it, but the truth is, we don't have time not to.

We have the opportunity every day to give generously from our experiences, share openly our trials and hard stuff, let others show up for us and take the time to show up for them. Everyone has their "junk," and the more we let people see ours, the more normal we all feel.

Freedom comes when we lay down our pride and recognize that having a need doesn't make us needy, it makes us human. If you called me today and said "Hey, we need to chat," or "Can we get together soon?" I'm going to make every effort to show up, to give generously to you whatever I have to give and connect with you on a personal level.

We all have relationships or friends for reasons, for seasons and for life. Whatever they are, we get to make the most of them today!

Who do you need to reach out to and spend time with in the next couple weeks?

_____
_____
_____
_____
_____
_____

Take time to write down your thoughts and needs in the area of relationships/friend-ships and begin to ask God to give you the strength and courage to pursue them.

_____
_____
_____
_____
_____
_____
_____
_____
_____
_____
_____
_____
_____
_____
_____
_____
_____
_____
_____
_____
_____
_____
_____
_____

Week Eight - Living in Relationships

Day Four - Healing Broken Relationships

We talked briefly in the last devotional about wounds and brokenness that come from relationships with others. Today we are going to do the heart work to allow God to mend some of those broken places for us.

When my daughter was little, she had a stuffed dog that she loved, and by loved, I mean, *loved*. This stuffed dog went everywhere with her. He was played with, and he looked like he had been through the sand box, literally. A family member offered to take her precious dog and clean him up a little. When she returned the stuffed dog to her, he looked brand new. Later in life, there was a season, after she had grown up some and her interests had changed, that this stuffed dog was nowhere to be found. We thought he was gone for good, but surprisingly, as we were cleaning out boxes in the attic getting ready for a move, that little stuffed dog showed up. He was placed back on the bed of the middle-schooler who had once abandoned her stuffed dog she used to love. This stuffed dog even went away with her to college, pinned to a bulletin board and hung in her closet. The same stuffed dog she once loved with a fierce toddler-love she now loves as an adult, knowing the hard things this stuffed animal has been through (a real-life puppy ripped an ear off that had to be sewn back on and chewed his nose off).

Real life relationships go through seasons and hardships, too. Friends or family that we fiercely love and even become dependent on can disappear from our lives, hurt, reject or disappoint us. We can lose touch with people, watch them get hurt and not be able to do anything about it, or push them away because they aren't meeting our needs anymore.

Rejection is real and painful. The opposite of rejection is acceptance. My identity isn't dependent on anyone's acceptance of me, and their identity isn't dependent on my acceptance of them. Often though, as we are hurting or broken, we hurt people.

The Lord is close to the brokenhearted and saves those who are crushed in spirit (Psalm 34:18 NIV).

The question isn't if we've been hurt by someone or if someone has hurt us because that's inevitable. The real question is, what are you going to do about it?

Think about a time recently when you've been hurt or offended by the words or actions of others. How did you handle it?

_____
_____
_____
_____

Now think about a time recently when you hurt or offended someone else by your words or actions. How did you handle that situation?

_____
_____
_____
_____

One of the greatest things I've learned in my journey is that life is too short to live offended. An offense is an event, but to be offended is a decision. Hurt or pride will often keep me from living in unity with my family, friends and brothers and sisters in Christ. The Word is clear that we are to forgive as we have been forgiven. Read Colossians 3:13, Matthew 6:14-15 and Luke 17:3-4. As you read through these verses, keep in mind the love and forgiveness we get to walk in every day. The same love and forgiveness we received we get to reciprocate and offer to others, whether we think they deserve it or not.

Here's a simple checklist for how to walk through an offense or hurt and heal broken relationships:

- Ask the Lord If there's anyone you are hurt or offended by.
    (1) What is the offense? What hurt or upset you?
    (2) Was it your personal interpretation, or did they actually say/do something against you?
    (3) Are you ready to forgive them and release them from their offense?
- Ask the Lord if there's anyone you have rejected, hurt or offended that you need to ask for forgiveness from.
    (1) Are you willing to go to the person and seek forgiveness?
    (2) Will they be open to you?

Sometimes there are things we have done or that have been done to us that we will never get the opportunity to be face-to-face with others to seek their forgiveness or receive their apology. In those situations, we get to forgive them by faith, even in their absence.

We've established this week that we must build our lives with God as our foundation. Loving ourselves is paramount to freely loving others. Loving others allows us to experience and give away the love of Jesus in a tangible way. There's freedom waiting for us as we release our grip. Many times, we are holding ourselves or others hostage by unforgiveness. We carry it with us, polluting or poisoning the relationship

FORGIVENESS IS...	FORGIVENESS ISN'T...
Letting go of the offense	Forgetting the offense ever happened
Releasing the offender from your resentment	Full restoration between the offended and the offender
Relinquishing your right to hold it against them	Dismissing the hurt or damage caused
Erasing the scoreboard	Condoning what happened
Freedom for the forgiver and the forgiven	Releasing the offender of their responsibility

As a team, we lead an outreach called Fully Alive. We serve together submitted to the Father. One thing we see more often than anything else is the damage caused by unforgiveness.

Through this ministry, we've seen that there are countless ways the enemy locks us up; however, one of the deadliest wounds that we see continuously is unforgiveness. Whether it comes from a spouse, coach, teacher, mom/dad or even a church leader, unforgiveness is poison to our soul.

Fear fueled from unforgiveness inhibits relationships. We get to be watchmen on the walls of our hearts identifying unforgiveness and seeking help from God and others to release that vice-grip that is suffocating our hearts and killing relationships.

When we are angry and fearful, we choke out the source of forgiveness for us. The mountain of unforgiveness separates us from God and some of the people we need most in our lives. As we acknowledge what Christ did on the cross, forgiving and remembering their sin no longer, we get to mimic that same act of love.

Our greatest pain and our greatest healing comes through people.

Take a minute and examine your heart and ask the Lord if there's any unforgiveness affecting your relationship with Him, with yourself or with others.

Do I have any unforgiveness towards God for anything He has allowed or hasn't done in my life?

_____

_____

_____

_____

Do I have any unforgiveness towards myself for anything I have/haven't done?

_____

_____

_____

_____

Do I have any unforgiveness towards someone else for something they have/haven't done?

_____

_____

_____

_____

After you have processed these questions, ask Holy Spirit if you are ready to forgive and release these offenses. It's ok if you're not. We know for some this takes time, and our sweet loving Father will guide you into all truth. We aren't going to walk this far together to ask you to complete a checklist. We will, however, ask you to continue to bring this before the Lord and to return to this place when you are ready.

If you're ready, we've included a simple prayer. Use this one or write out your own. Either way He is glorified as we trust Him with the hurt and broken pieces of our hearts and our lives.

Lord,

Thank you for loving me right where I am. Thank you that Your desire is always to help me go deeper and to trust you more. Today I realize that I hold unforgiveness towards _____
I choose to forgive, releasing _____
from the offense of_____
I will no longer allow this to rob me of my peace and trust in You. Thank you that I can release this, and I don't have to carry the weight of it any longer. You are bigger and stronger than I, and today I choose to receive and walk in your love and forgiveness, modeled on the cross and offered every day.

In Jesus name, Amen.

Here are a few deadly relationship killers.Circle the ones that are robbing your relationships. We get to evaluate all of our relationships and examine our hearts and motives. As we continue to be led by the Holy Spirit, grace, love and truth we learn to weed out all counterfeits. It is God's desire to bring freedom, peace and ultimately joy in place of the things above. Many times, we already know where we've partnered with something that doesn't line up with Him or His love. We choose as sons and daughters to walk courageously releasing these deadly snares of the enemy affecting our relationships.

Week Eight - Living in Relationships

Day Five - Living Like Relationships Matter

Every day I get to make a choice to live like today matters. My choices matter. My relationships matter. My life matters. My faith-walk matters. My family matters. God matters, and people matter. All of it, every bit of it is significant and plays a part in me living my best life.

Jesus said in the second half of John 10:10 (NIV) that *"I have come that you may have life and have it to the full."* Some translations say abundant life or rich and satisfying life, a life in all its fullness.

A full life is not a happy, care-free, problem-free life. **A full life is one lived with intention, maximizing every moment and cherishing the ones that matter most while making the most of the opportunities laid before you every day.**

In light of everything you've read, studied and learned on our journey together, take a few minutes and write out what you would call a full life.

_____

_____

_____

_____

We want to wrap up our time together by writing our own personal manifesto. A manifesto is simply a public declaration of policy and aims. Essentially, it's your truth declaration about your relationship with God, yourself and others. It's a declaration of the aim of your life. Zig Ziglar said, "If you aim for nothing, you'll hit it every-time."

elevateHim Team Manifesto:

Our relationship with the Father, Son and Holy Spirit is our most important investment.

We will be real, raw and transparent in our relationship with the Father, ourselves and each other, speaking truth motivated by love and spurring each other on to Christ-likeness.

We will give grace no matter what; we will believe the best in each other and others because we are in this together.

We will be about unity; handling offenses swiftly and forgiving generously.

If we work at anything, we will work at rest and make it a priority to go to the Word and Go to the Woods to hear God for ourselves and this ministry.

We have full permission to be ourselves, failing forward to learn and grow, living in transparency and vulnerability.

We will honor the Lord and each other; serving the team, surrendered to the process and submitted to authority.

Our greatest honor comes as we honor the Lord, each other and His Kingdom government!

So take a few minutes and brainstorm things that are important to you or what you're aiming for to be your personal "policy." After you've written some things down, put numbers beside them ranking them in importance to you. Finally, use the last page to write out your personal manifesto for life. To take it a step further, we invite you to post it on social media and tag @elevateHim. We are cheering you on, praying for you and are honored to be a part of this journey with you.

My Personal Manifesto:

_____
_____
_____
_____
_____
_____
_____
_____
_____
_____
_____
_____
_____
_____
_____
_____
_____
_____
_____
_____
_____

Week Eight - Living in Relationships

Day Six - Resting in Peace

Peace I leave with you; my peace I give you. I do not give to you as the world gives. Do not let your hearts be troubled and do not be afraid (John 14:27 NIV).

His peace never leaves us. We can allow things, situations and people to disrupt our peace. On the flip side, we can choose to pursue peace.

Turn away from evil and do good. Search for peace, and work to maintain it (Psalm 34:14 NLT).

We've talked a lot about work and rest. Our motto at elevateHim is "If we work at anything, work at rest." Peace is synonymous with rest. Rest impacts every relationship in our lives. When we are burned-out or worn-out, the people we love most get our leftovers, or worse, the emotional explosion will splash all over them.

We talked this week about the importance of a healthy relationship with God, ourselves and others. There are some hard things we've asked you to do as you forgive and release others from the offenses you've held against them.

We hope that you've not only read this book, but that we have created opportunities for you to experience and live out what we are unpacking, and that we are creating a new belief system together that ultimately impacts our behavior. Right believing produces right behavior!

His peace trumps any situation we go through. He promises is to never leave us or forsake us. Today, your task is simple. I want to ask you to engage in a life-giving relationship. Ask the Holy Spirit to show you someone you can spend time with, whether it's your spouse, one of your children or a friend or relative. Set aside a time to get together with them and just talk. Being face-to-face with people I love and who love me speaks rest to my soul.

Because we were created to live out our faith in the context of community, it's important to practice living in community. We can't get good at something we aren't willing to invest in or practice. Be intentional and make it a priority!

Ask the Holy Spirit to activate the peace that Jesus gives you as you engage with the people around you. Be present, be willing and be ready for God to bless you through them!

From the team at elevateHim, this is our prayer for you.

May the LORD bless you and keep you;
the LORD make His face to shine upon you and be gracious to you;
the LORD lift up His countenance upon you and give you peace.
Numbers 6:24-26 NIV

This is a final declaration written for you. Read it out loud and as you read it, receive it as truth, your truth, and commit to living like you believe it.

Dear Brothers and Sisters,

You are loved by the Father, the Son and the Holy Spirit who are three-in-one at work and moving on your behalf. You are fully equipped because of the grace of God given to you freely through the cross, to love and live loved.

You have everything you need to teach you, guide you and lead you through the Word, His love-letter to you. You are more than able to hear His voice, know Him intimately and experience the relational dialog He desires, and you need.

The cross was God's love demonstrated for you to see that in the midst of pain, God's love remains steadfast, unwavering and immovable. Sin is the enemy, but the grace and love of the Father, revealed through Jesus and deposited in you through the Holy Spirit, can conquer any and all enemies. Your identity is firmly rooted in the truth that you are His: chosen, treasured, dearly loved and fully equipped for everything you walk through and everything He calls you to.

Each and every relationship in your life provides an opportunity for you to pursue Christ-like-ness, share truth and embody love to a fallen and broken world from inside the walls of your own home to the ends of the earth. Grace is God's gift to you, through the love of God on display through the life of Jesus and the Holy Spirit at work in and through you.

You can do this, you will do this, you are doing this, and we are so proud of you and honored to be on the journey with you as we learn and grow together!

With love,
The elevateHim Team

Appendix

Salvation Letter

Dear Friends,

Number one, if you are reading this, there is a huge group of people celebrating with you. The angels in heaven are celebration your new birth as you move from death to life. This is an important day, write it down! Your name is now written in the Lamb's Book of Life.

We've talked about salvation, but we wouldn't be a good brother or sister if we didn't walk with you and show you how to accept the gift of salvation. Salvation is a free gift from God, given to us because of the death of His Son Jesus. It's an act of choice, choosing to lay aside your old life and walking in your new identity as a chosen and dearly loved child of God.

Now, read through this scripture Romans 10:9-11.

- Confess Jesus as Lord of your life.
- Believe God raised Him from the dead.
- Receive the gift of eternal life and the fullness of God the Father, Son and Holy Spirit in your life.

It really is that simple. There are no special words reserved for certain people to make this "official". God did that for us through Jesus, and you are now fully equipped to live as a child of God. You inherit the promise of eternity in heaven with our Creator and experience the fullness of life and the power of the Holy Spirit at work in and through you.

Welcome to the family! We can't wait to watch God work and move in and through you! If you made this decision and prayed to receive salvation we would love to connect with you. You can contact us by emailing info@elevateHim.com.

> With love,
> *The elevateHim Team*

Baptism

There are two main ordinances (religious rituals) of the early Church that we still practice today, Baptism and Communion. Baptism is simply an outward representation of an inward decision. Once you have declared Jesus as Lord of your life and believed in your heart God raised Him from the dead, the scriptures tell us we are saved. Before Jesus ever set out in His ministry He was baptized, setting an example for every believer to follow. Just as we wear a wedding ring to symbolize the commitment made to our spouse, we are baptized to publicly share of the life-giving gift we were given through salvation. Baptism, by immersion, is a representation of the death and burial of our old self who is now raised with new life through Christ.

Baptism usually happens in the local church and we encourage you to reach out to your church to find out more. If you are not connected to a church yet and would like us to help we are glad to share with you our recommendations for local churches or help you in your search for a church home.

You can contact us at: **info@elevateHim.com**.

Your Guide to Communion

Communion is another practice from the early church that Jesus modeled, and we observe regularly. For some, communion is a daily, weekly, monthly or periodic opportunity to remember and celebrate what God has done, is doing and will do.

The covenant He made with us through Jesus sealed the deal for eternity and opened the door wide open. We take communion to celebrate what Jesus did for us. It was modeled by Jesus himself and we follow his example because we love Him and because we are loved by Him.

But, communion isn't something reserved for specific times, day or places. Breaking bread is something we can do in our homes, at restaurants, with our families and our community. It's also something we can do one-on-one in the privacy of our intimate time with our Creator over coffee and a donut. We've given you simple instructions to use as a guide when you want to take communion by yourself, with your family, or with your community.

- Grab whatever you have that's a solid and a liquid (seriously). It can be a piece of toast, a cracker, a chip, whatever it is can be symbolic of the breaking of bread as Jesus did in the Upper Room for the Last Supper.

- Grab your cup of water, juice or soda that symbolizes His blood shed for you and me.

- As you break and eat the bread (solid) thank Him for what He did on the cross, but don't stop at that. Take a minute and thank Him for the life you have now because of the Cross, what HE IS DOING and ways that He is working and moving on your behalf right now. It's not about a special prayer with rehearsed words but your heart expressed through gratitude to His throne offered through grace.

- As you drink the cup (liquid) take time to remember the final covenant between God and us through the shed blood of Jesus on the cross. Thank Him for the redemption, healing, protection and provision He provides and the direct access that we now have that we can commune with God on a personal level because of what Jesus accomplished through the cross and resurrection.

That's it! Plain and simple. There's no wrong or right way if your heart is to remember and honor the Father for what He did through Jesus for us and direct our attention towards what He is still at work doing in and through us.

Every time we break bread in our homes we give thanks and remember and invite you into the regular practice as well. We would love to hear your stories so if you want to share about a special time of communion send us an email info@elevate-Him.com. Praying for each of you!

Every day they continued to meet together in the temple courts. They broke bread in their homes and ate together with glad and sincere hearts,
Acts 2:46 NIV

Fully Alive Events

Based on Proverbs 4:23- *"Above all else guard your heart for out of the heart flow all the issues of life"*, Fully Alive is an event where we set aside a few days to allow God to speak to the hearts and lives of men and women. It's a time dedicated to allowing men and women to find their true identity, purpose and destiny while connecting intimately with their loving Father. We purposefully do not share any of the details of the Fully Alive weekend for the those who are considering attending. If the world can keep a secret, then we can keep it sacred. Everyone's Fully Alive story is different but shares the commonality that it is a sacred time where God speaks and moves in ways that transforms individuals, marriages, families, churches, communities and relationships. For some this is a leap of faith, but as Romans 1:17 says; "…it is through faith that a righteous person has life."

For more information about Fully Alive events
or elevateHim Ministries.
You can contact us at:

www.elevatehim.com
P.O. Box 2554
Fort Worth, TX 76244
(817) 431-3336

181